Red Cloud's War: The History and Legacy of the Only 19th Century War Won by Native Americans against the United States

By Charles River Editors

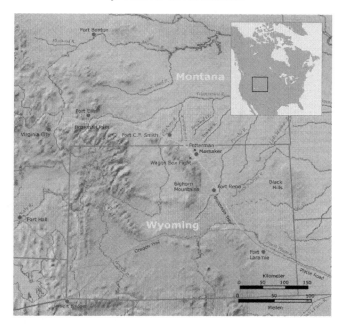

An 1860s depiction of the Bozeman Trail

About Charles River Editors

Charles River Editors is a boutique digital publishing company, specializing in bringing history back to life with educational and engaging books on a wide range of topics. Keep up to date with our new and free offerings with this 5 second sign up on our weekly mailing list, and visit Our Kindle Author Page to see other recently published Kindle titles.

We make these books for you and always want to know our readers' opinions, so we encourage you to leave reviews and look forward to publishing new and exciting titles each week.

Introduction

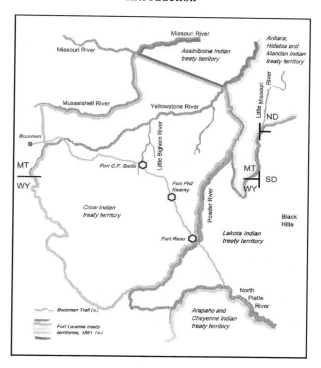

A map of the contested region

Red Cloud's War

"When the Great Father at Washington sent us his chief soldier to ask for a path through our hunting grounds, a way for his iron road to the mountains and the western sea, we were told that they wished merely to pass through our country, not to tarry among us, but to seek for gold in the far west. Our old chiefs thought to show their friendship and good will, when they allowed this dangerous snake in our midst. They promised to protect the wayfarers. Yet before the ashes of the council fire are cold, the Great Father is building his forts among us. You have heard the sound of the white soldier's ax upon the Little Piney. His presence here is an insult and a threat. It is an insult to the spirits of our ancestors. Are we then to give up their sacred graves to be plowed for corn? Dakotas, I am for war!" – Red Cloud

Even before the American Revolution, Americans traveled west. From the narrow strip of the

13 colonies, across the Appalachians, ever westward they journeyed, and by the end of the 19th century, the United States of America stretched from sea to shining sea.

Of course, just because the names on the borders changed, it did not tame the land or its previous residents. Americans desired California and Oregon, going to war for one and nearly going to war for the other. Once acquired, it now fell to the salt of the earth to settle these claimed lands, and everything in between. To do this meant crossing terrain unused to the heavy traffic of Westerners on the move.

Though Indian trails followed rivers, hills, and valleys across the plains, Westerners often needed to create new paths capable of handling the heaver traffic and bulky covered wagons. At the same time, safety often required avoiding the natives. Though sometimes co-opting Indian trails for this purpose, oftentimes pioneering settlers worked to avoid such routes as well, especially when the natives took exception to their new neighbors.

From this need came two adventurers determined to find a path north to the latest gold rush at the end of the road. Though such trails already existed, these two men forged a new trail, one that would bring a great deal of woe to the local natives. Why build such a trail through such a tumultuous land, exacerbating already tenuous relations with the natives and even souring those of the few the United States could call allies? As is often the case with such questions, the answer begins with geography, the greatest boon and bane to adventurers since mankind first started traveling.

The Bozeman Trail ran through the Powder River country, which included the traditional hunting grounds of Lakota, Cheyenne, and Arapaho peoples. Attempts by the natives to prevent encroachment and armed defense of settlers along the trail led to conflicts in short order. Shortly after the Civil War, the U.S. found itself engaged against the Sioux in what came to be known as Red Cloud's War. Among the Oglala Lakota, one of the most famous bands of the Native American Tribe known as the Sioux, Red Cloud led the group for 40 years, in war, in peace, and on a reservation, becoming so esteemed and influential that Americans began to mistakenly take him for the leader of the entire Sioux tribe.

In the summer of 1866, Colonel Henry B. Carrington set out from Fort Laramie to establish a series of forts along the Bozeman Trail with the goal of protecting migrants moving along the trail. The Bozeman Trail ran through the Powder River country, which included the traditional hunting grounds of Lakota, Cheyenne, and Arapaho peoples. Carrington had about 1,000 people in his column, of which about 700 were soldiers and 300 were civilians, likely soldiers' families and migrants.

The colonel established Fort Phil Kearny as his headquarters and based 400 troops and most of the civilians there. During the construction of Fort Kearny, which lasted months, Native Americans killed several dozen soldiers and civilians in some 50 separate attacks. The attacks were largely focused on the "wood trains", comprised of soldiers and civilians harvesting lumber from the surrounding forest for the construction of the fort. Though younger warriors like Crazy Horse conducted the actual attack, Red Cloud and other, older leaders would help plan and direct the harassment and interdiction campaign against the construction of Fort Kearny.

By October 1866, Carrington's officers and men pressured him to go on the offensive and take the fight to the Native Americans. The pressure was increased by the arrival of a company of sixty-three cavalry troopers led by Lieutenant Horatio S. Bingham in early November. Civil War veterans Captain William J. Fetterman and Captain James W. Powell accompanied the cavalry troopers and were assigned to Fort Kearny as infantry officers, but despite having a distinguished war record, Fetterman had no experience fighting Native Americans. Nevertheless, that lack of experience did not keep Fetterman from criticizing the conservative and defensive posture Carrington had established at Fort Kearny, adding to an already growing chorus of criticism. Fetterman also repeatedly displayed utter contempt for the Native Americans.

In late November, Carrington received orders from his commander, General Philip St. George Cooke, to take the offensive against the Native Americans. The first opportunity for offensive action came on December 6, when pickets reported that a wood train four miles from the fort was under attack. The attack was however, merely a feint, meant to lure troops into a Native American ambush. Carrington ordered Fetterman to take a company of cavalry, bolstered by a squad of mounted infantry, to relieve the wood train. Meanwhile, Carrington would lead a mounted squad to the north to cut off the Native Americans' presumed escape route.

On December 19, another wood train was attacked, and Carrington dispatched a mixed company of cavalry and mounted infantry led by Captain Powell. This time, the cautious officer followed Carrington explicit orders not to pursue the Native Americans over the ridge and out of sight of the fort. Powell was successful and returned to the fort unscathed. Carrington continued to emphasize the need for caution until reinforcements and horse arrived from Fort Laramie. Two days later, Native Americans again attacked a wood train, and Carrington dispatched a mixed force of about 50 infantrymen and nearly 30 cavalry troopers and Colonel Carrington again chose Captain Powell to lead the relieving force, but Fetterman asserted his seniority to Powell and was thus given command of the soldiers. Again, Carrington ordered the troops not to pursue the warriors over the nearby ridge and out of sight of the fort.

When Fetterman left the fort, he immediately disobeyed orders and took the trail that followed the ridgeline. The Colonel assumed that Fetterman was planning to attack the warriors from the north; instead, he and his force disappeared over the ridge. At this point the attack on the wood train ended and about 50 warriors attacked the fort but were repelled by a few cannon shots.

Meanwhile, the Native American warriors had deployed a group of decoying riders, including Crazy Horse, who lured Fetterman's troops over the ridge and into the waiting ambush. About midday, soldiers at Fort Kearny heard a large volume of gunfire coming from the north, the direction where Fetterman had led his troops. Carrington dispatched 75 troops towards the gunfire and soon afterwards sent another 48. About an hour later, as the troops topped the ridgeline, they saw a group of some 1,000 warriors in the valley below. Warriors approached and taunted the soldiers, but soon they began to disperse and disappear. Captain Ten Eyck, leading the relief force, cautiously moved onto the battlefield and found Fetterman and his men dead, stripped, and mutilated. Until that time, the Fetterman Massacre, as U.S. newspapers labeled the event, was the greatest defeat (in terms of the number of U.S. soldiers killed) experienced by the

Army at the hands of Native American warriors.

The ongoing hostilities ultimately convinced American officials to head back to the negotiating table with the Native Americans, and as a result, Red Cloud has often been labeled the only Indian chief to win a war against the Americans. After that, however, Red Cloud continued to lead his people to reservations first near the Black Hills and later westward after the Battle of the Little Bighorn. Though he was respected as a war chief, it was his political functions as a spokesman of the Oglala that truly allowed Red Cloud to leave his mark over the last several decades of his life. Whereas Sitting Bull and Crazy Horse suffered premature deaths, Red Cloud outlived the other important leaders of the Sioux until dying in 1909 at 87 years old. Near the end of his life, he reportedly said, "They made us many promises, more than I can remember. But they kept but one -- they promised to take our land...and they took it."

Red Cloud's War: The History and Legacy of the Only 19th Century War Won by Native Americans against the United States analyzes the seminal moments that brought about the war, the war's most famous battles, and the aftermath. Along with pictures depicting important people, places, and events, you will learn about Red Cloud's War like never before.

Red Cloud's War: The History and Legacy of the Only 19th Century War Won by Native Americans against the United States

Relations with Native Americans

From the late 1830s onward, the tenor of intertribal warfare began to change, as more lethal weaponry (firearms) became common among Native American warriors. The sheer deadliness of these new weapons had a grave impact on Plains peoples, as killing enemies became relatively easy. The availability of firearms and liquor, both provided by the European-American settlers and traders, would also make Native Americans a more formidable enemy for the whites.

In 1851, General William S. Harney convened a meeting, calling all western Sioux bands to Fort Laramie to negotiate territorial and "right-of-way" issues through their territory. United States officials wanted the Sioux to end their custom of intertribal warfare to achieve Harney's goal of allowing settlers to pass through the region in safety. As a result, the general was ordered to obtain permission from the Native American leaders for settlers traveling through Sioux lands en route to the Pacific coast. This became even more imperative when the California Gold Rush of 1849 led that many more people west in search of riches.

General Harney

The government solution was to assign each band a defined territory where they were to remain, but such types of negotiation were meaningless to the Sioux, who failed to see the validity made without the consensus of all involved. The Oglalas especially viewed the negotiations with suspicion and were largely uninterested in the outcome. Red Cloud and his relatives were uninvolved in the proceeding until one Oglala leader, Bear Bull, was plied with liquor and persuaded to advocate for the treaty among his fellow Oglalas. The old chief strongly argued for the treaty and even sought to dictate the actions of his people. His attempt was a complete and utter failure, and his drunken response was a rash decision to fire into a crowd of his own people, during which he killed Red Cloud's father and brother.

In the warrior societies of the Plains, it fell upon Red Cloud to avenge the deaths of his relatives, and with a stolid nature born from a knowledge of and faith in his way of life, Red Cloud challenged Bear Bull. In the ensuing challenge, Red Cloud shot and killed both Bear Bull and his son, who had tried to defend his inebriated father. While this outcome seemed harsh and tragic, Red Cloud's actions were supported by his people; he had done what was expected of an Oglala warrior.

Eventually, the Fort Laramie Treaty of 1851 was signed between the Americans and representatives for several Native American tribes, including the Cheyenne, Sioux, Arapaho, Crow, Assiniboine, Mandan, Hidatsa, and Arikara. The treaty offered tribes an annuity payment to allow white settlers access to move westward across the Oregon Trail, and the treaty effectively created and defined the territory of each participating band with the intent of ending the traditional warfare between different Sioux bands. While the Native Americans consented to the creation of roads and even forts along the route, they did not consent to settlers encroaching on the lands marked for them, which would inevitably happen as the federal government turned a blind eye.

As a result of the treaty, various warriors were designated "chiefs" by the government officials drafting the document, regardless of the actual influence they had among their people. That was hardly the only problem, because by the mid-1850s, the Fort Laramie Treaty of 1851 had been rendered largely meaningless. Lakota and Dakota Sioux bands who were unaware of the existence of the treaty continued their traditional and annual raiding against other Native American bands, and white settlers and migrants continually trespassed through Sioux territory in violation of the treaty's stipulations.

In 1854, various Sioux bands were encamped near Fort Laramie when an emaciated cow wandered into the mixed Lakota camp where Red Cloud and Spotted Tail were living. In such mixed gatherings, Native Americans assumed a very forgiving and conciliatory attitude toward one another, a politeness that sought to avoid unnecessary conflict. A Miniconjou warrior named High Forehead soon slaughtered and processed the animal, but it turned out the bovine had escaped from a Mormon wagon train migrating west. Shortly after, the animal's owner approached Lieutenant John Fleming, the senior officer at Fort Laramie, reporting that Native Americans had stolen his cow.

Chief Spotted Tail

Fleming summoned Conquering Bear to the fort to discuss the matter, because Conquering Bear was the Brule Lakota warrior who had been arbitrarily named a "chief" by the American representatives during the Fort Laramie treaty council in 1851. They had demanded a single representative from each group with which to deal, and when the indigenous people did not acknowledge a single leader, they appointed leaders for them. When Conquering Bear arrived at Fort Laramie, he tried to negotiate compensation for the cow, offering several ponies from his personal herd or a cow from the band's herd, understanding that the conditions of the Fort Laramie Treaty rendered this matter to the Indian Agent. The Mormon migrant refused these offers and instead demanded $25, and Lieutenant Fleming gave in to the Mormon demand that the offending Native American, High Forehead, be arrested. To do so he dispatched his subordinate to the Lakota camp to arrest the offending warrior. Second Lieutenant John L. Grattan was ready and willing to lead a force to arrest High Forehead, but both he and his commander were unaware that these types of matters had been delegated to the local Indian Agent and were not the purview of the military.

A photo of Fort Laramie in the 1850s

The appointed agent had not yet arrived in the area, so on August 29, 1854, Grattan led a force of twenty-nine soldiers, interpreter Lucien Auguste, and two cannons to the Lakota encampment. Auguste was greatly disliked by the Lakota and drank heavily on the way to the camp, arriving very drunk. As the soldiers entered the camp, Auguste began taunting the warriors, calling them women and saying that the soldiers had come to kill, not to negotiate. Grattan broke Auguste's bottle and openly berated him, indicating that he likely understood the danger of the situation his force faced. The encampment was populated by an estimated 4,800 mixed Lakota people and about 1,200 warriors.

James Bordeaux, who owned the nearby trading post, was consulted and advised Lieutenant Grattan to speak directly with Conquering Bear and allow the Native American leadership to handle the situation. Although Bordeaux reported that Grattan seemed to understand, the young, recent West Point graduate went directly to High Forehead's lodge and demanded his surrender. When High Forehead refused, Grattan then went to Conquering Bear and demanded that he hand over High Forehead. The warrior refused because he had no authority over the Miniconjou and did not want to violate the tradition of hospitality extended to visitors from other bands.

The negotiations went on for some time, with the drunken Auguste speaking broken Dakota (since he had no knowledge of other dialects). As Grattan pushed Conquering Bear to hand over High Forehead, warriors moved into flanking positions around the soldiers. Exasperated, Grattan ended the discussion and began walking back to his column. As he walked, one of the nervous troops fired a shot that struck a Lakota warrior. Chaos ensued and a firefight broke out, during which Conquering Bear was shot in the back and died nine days later. Grattan, Auguste, and the rest of the soldiers were soon dead. As the fight progressed a group of about eighteen soldiers tried to break out and reach the safety of some nearby rocks, but they were run down and killed by a group of warriors led by Red Cloud. The enraged Native Americans then looted the trading post but did not hurt Bordeaux, whom they regarded as a friend.

Naturally, the "Grattan Massacre" became a catalyst for a generalized hostility between whites and Lakota people that would last for over two decades, but despite the obvious implications of the Grattan Massacre, at first there was no real reaction or retribution from the U.S. Army and government. Intertribal warfare between Sioux bands and their Cheyenne and Arapaho enemies resumed around 1860.

The Bozeman Trail

Though there was some debate after its founding regarding the trail's length, the Bozeman Trail's accepted start is Fort Laramie in Wyoming and ending at Virginia City, Montana. Ironically, in order to aid in westward travel, the Bozeman Trail actually traveled east.

A photo of Fort Laramie in the 1850s

The Bozeman Trail itself was based on older trails long-trodden by local Indians, and is not only easily navigable, but well-watered and foraged, crossing six large rivers including the North Platte, both Bighorns, Yellowstone, and finally the Missouri River. Thanks to these rivers and relatively flat land well grassed, the trail's selection is easy enough to see from a geographic sense, especially taking into account the skirting of the nearby Bighorn Mountains.

Forging a trail through such open lands takes time, of course, and as is usual when the whites and natives clashed, a great deal of blood was shed. At the same time, before the Bozeman Trail had its name, a very similar path was used by the natives, who, as time would tell, did not like sharing their road with uninvited guests, especially ones who stuck around long after their welcome.

Long before men from Europe even knew there was land west of the Mississippi to covet, the natives had long traveled well-worn paths through nature. Like the old roads before interstates, these routes moved with the land, allowing travelers to water, forage, and rest when they needed to without veering from the trail. The Bozeman Trail was no exception to this rule, and that's what caused such problems.

The local natives, residing in the Powder River Country traversed by what would become the Bozeman Trail, were originally the Crows. Such was their association with the land that early fur traders of the time called the land what the crows called themselves: Absaroka.[i] A Crow chief once said to a trader in the region, "There is no country like Crow country."[ii] A trader long used to the area said in 1855 that the land was "perhaps the best game country in the world."[iii]

Inevitably, that land was desired by other tribes being forced westward by advancing white settlers, and as the 19th century wore on, the Crows would find several tribes encroaching on their lands along with whites.

The Bozeman Trail would only exacerbate these issues, but before it existed, few whites traveled through the region. Most people traveling west either followed the Missouri River to Fort Benton, or took the southern route from Salt Lake City, one of the earliest routes west across the Great Plains.[iv] Both of these routes had their own issues –the Missouri River became a favored ambush point of the Sioux, and the Salt Lake Route was 450 miles longer than what would become the Bozeman Trail. Further, traversing the Salt Lake Route risked traveling through the Salt Lake itself, and doing so with poor planning or simple bad luck could spell doom for any enterprising settler.[v]

Most of the traders before the opening of the Trail were fur traders, and that trade grew critical for the Crows as time passed. So, too, did the trade for firearms, as the nearby tribes put pressure on Crow lands augmented by weapons purchased by traders.[vi] While fur and firearms traders were welcome, gold prospectors were not, and unfortunately it was the latest gold rush that brought two failed prospectors to search for a new route north.[vii]

Two failed prospectors traversing these lands would forge a new era in relations, and in the process they would attempt to establish a new trail safe from Sioux raids. Their names were John Jacobs and John Bozeman.[viii]

JOHN M. BOZEMAN
Pathbreaker of the Bozeman Trail.

Bozeman

At that time, traveling west from the settled land east and along the Mississippi River before the continent-spanning railroads was dangerous at best, foolhardy at worse. Indian raids, hostile land, and long, unending nothing hounded the brave souls traveling west like vultures, which also circled above when not on the ground pecking on the latest hapless traveler. To protect themselves and their wares or supplies, traders and settlers started traveling in great wagon trains, utilizing the strength of numbers to travel in something resembling safety.[ix] Prior to the Oregon Trail, many settlers and traders utilized the older Santa Fe Trail, where these wagon caravan pioneers dug the first great wagon grooves into the land.[x] The more northern Oregon Trail suited the needs of those traveling to the new northwestern lands, whereas the Santa Fe Trail ended, unsurprisingly, at Santa Fe, New Mexico, from whence the settlers and traders heading west would find themselves in southern California. By the 1840s, the Oregon Trail was a major road for settlers, branching off as needed to the north and south to link up with the remains of older trails.[xi]

Slowly, the Oregon Trail acquired forts and other posts for those using it to resupply and find shelter if needed, thus creating one of the greatest western routes in American history. What the nation lacked, however, was a link from this great trail to the northern plains, a land rich in resources but just as difficult to travel as the west. It was this dream for a northern trail that compelled Bozeman and Jacobs on their journey.

Their journey began from Bannack, a bustling mining camp in the Montana Territory. In the winter of 1862, they set out from Montana southward to find a shorter route for prospective miners and settlers.[xii] The customary routes for such pioneers involved either heading north up the Missouri River, or west on the Oregon Trail until heading north at Fort Hall, then onward to Virginia City. Both routes were long and risked the ire of the locals.[xiii]

Bozeman and Jacobs' adventure reads much like any great exploration story of the Great Plains. Barely had they set out before hostile Sioux took their horses and supplies, forcing them to face the open winter landscape on foot. Somehow they survived to reach the Missouri River, and in the spring of 1863, their fortunes turned for the better.[xiv] Commandeering a wagon train, Bozeman set out to retrace his steps in an effort to find his new trail. West of Fort Laramie, in lands that would someday hold that promised trail, he once again ran into the locals who declared he and his wagon train had no right to cross their land. Forced to withdraw, this seemingly innocuous encounter was but the first clash of whites and natives within the lands of the Bozeman Trail.[xv] The wagon train proceeded to take the long way to Montana, but Bozeman did not join them. Determined to find his route, he and a small group of adventurous, deranged, or highly paid explorers pushed north from the North Platte River into hostile lands.[xvi] Traveling by night to avoid Indian scouts, the small group pushed across the lands to forge a new path northward. Eventually, the group reached the divide between the Bridger and Gallatin mountain ranges, and one of Bozeman's fellow explorers named the discovered divide Bozeman Pass.[xvii]

ROCK CANYON NEAR BOZEMAN, M.T.

A 19th century depiction of Bozeman Pass

Thanks to the token military presence in the area at the time, there is an intriguing account of

Bozeman's trailblazing efforts, a story that many would not find out of place in the works of Edgar Allen Poe. U.S. Army Captain James Stuart recalled, "Looking across the river, about a mile above us, I saw three white men with six horses, three packed, three riding. They were coming down the river and I waited until they got opposite of us and then hailed them. They would neither answer nor stop, but kept the same course and at a little faster pace. I then sent Underwood and Stone across ahead of our pack train to overtake them and hear the news …We started to meet the strangers, not doubting but our men had overtaken them…We met our men re-turning without having seen anything of the travelers… We followed them for ten miles and then gave up the chase. It seems that as soon as they got out of our sight, they had started on a run, and kept in ravines and brush along the creek for about three miles till they got into the hills… We found that we could not overtake them. We found a fry pan and a pack of cards on their trail. None of us have the least idea who they are, where they come from or where they were going."[xviii]

As it turned out, the three riders were Bozeman, his partner, and Bozeman's three-year old daughter, proving once again it takes a certain something to be a trailblazer.[xix] Concerned about Indian scouts, the small group avoided Stuart's men out of fear of a native assault. Eccentricities aside, the lands described in the above quote would come to be the Jacobs' and Bozeman Cut-off, or, as it later became known, the Bozeman Trail.[xx]

Of course, naming a trail is all well and good, but if no one actually uses the trail, it is no better than a path the natives had exclusive claim to anyway. In 1864, Bozeman gathered a wagon train in Missouri and set out along his newly named trail. Meanwhile, a fellow trailblazer by the name of Jim Bridger, competing with Bozeman, gathered his own wagon train and set out on a different path, believing Bozeman's route too difficult to traverse.[xxi] Now one of the West's most famous mountain men, Bridger took a route following a more curving, western road that took him up and down several rivers and creeks in the region, and though he beat Bozeman to the Yellowstone River, one of the checkpoints along the path, he also had a head start of several weeks.[xxii] Bozeman's more direct route led him to the Gallatin Valley ahead of Bridger, and the two wagon trains actually reached Virginia City only hours apart.[xxiii] Ultimately, Bozeman's Trail, which was shorter, better watered and with game aplenty, became the major trail.

Bridger

Bozeman set out again in 1864 with another train, and slowly the road came into steady use. For the next several years, the trail saw limited but regular use by homesteaders, traders, and prospectors.[xxiv] One of the largest of these trains traversed the route in 1864, consisting of 156 wagons carrying 369 men, 36 women, 56, children, 636 oxen, 194 cows, 79 horses, and 12 mules.[xxv]

These were the great wagon trains envisioned by Bozeman and the whole purpose of blazing his trail, but the Bozeman Trail itself could be a nebulous entity, thanks to the open nature of the terrain. Though a broad line across the Plains can be pointed to as the Bozeman Trail, the route's specific path seemed to be somewhat contentious during its brief life.[xxvi] Several Army commanders in the area each had their own idea of the Trail's specifics at various points, and it is from these varied routes that the Trail as a whole comes together. Based on its later importance for the soldiers stuck defending it, one path for the Bozeman Trail began in Fort Kearny, Nebraska (not to be confused with the later Fort Phil Kearny on the Trail proper).[xxvii] From there, the Trail headed west to Fort McPherson, then, 110 miles later, Fort Sedgwick, considered by one local Army officer the true start of the Trail, traveling mostly west but occasionally dipping

south or north to Fort Laramie.[xxviii]

Fort Kearny

This version of the Bozeman Trail ran substantially longer than the generally accepted path, and it mixed with the Oregon Trail at several locations. A more commonly accepted route starts at Fort Laramie, traveling mostly northwest until reaching the few forts built along the Trail for its protection.[xxix]

Thanks to the surveys made of the Trail, there are very detailed descriptions of the Bozeman Trail proper, and accurate records of its length. Beginning the Trail at the generally accepted start of Fort Laramie, the distances between the forts are as follows:

Fort Laramie to Fort Reno 169
From Fort Reno to Fort Phil Kearny 67
From Fort Phil Kearny to Fort C. F. Smith 91
From Fort C. F. Smith to Virginia City 281[xxx]

This puts the overall length of the Bozeman Trail at 608 miles. The generally accepted length of the Trail tends to be around this length, and not the much longer version starting in Nebraska.

Despite its naming and the beginning of its usage, Bozeman's Trail was not strictly legal, certainly not during the initial part of its brief life. This is because it crossed lands that were ceded to the natives and thus were part of their sovereign territory. The natives naturally took umbrage with the whites yet again flouting their own treaties and agreements.[xxxi] The Americans, in turn, pointed to an amended version of the treaty signed at Fort Laramie in 1851, concerning those natives who were "residing south of the Missouri River, east of the Rocky Mountains, and north of the lines of Texas and New Mexico, viz, the Sioux or Dahcotas, Cheyennes, Arappahoes, Crows, Assinaboines, Gros-Ventre, Mandans, and Arrickara…"[xxxii] Pointing specifically to Article Two of the treaty, it stated, "The aforesaid nations do hereby recognize the right of the United States Government to establish roads, military and other posts, within their respective territories."[xxxiii] The treaty also established the borders of the Crow Indians, consisting of the lands around the Yellowstone River and its tributary, the Powder River. In other words, the Bozeman Trail legally ran through Crow territory, at least according to the American government.

At the time, the Crows were one of the friendlier natives in the region, thanks in part to the fact the U.S. came to their defense against the more hostile Blackfeet and Sioux. The Sioux in particular often raided against the Crows - and Americans for that matter - an issue that would come to a boil sooner rather than later.[xxxiv]

For Bozeman himself, sooner turned out to be mid-April in 1867. Having set out with a partner by the name of Tom Coover, they headed down the Yellowstone River to Fort C. F. Smith, only to have their horses stolen by raiding Indians. The next day, the two encountered more natives, whom Bozeman believed to be friendly Crows, but they were actually exiled Blackfeet residing with the Crows. The Blackfeet shot Bozeman twice, killing him.[xxxv]

The Bozeman Trail's trailblazer and namesake lay dead, and his partner demanded retribution. In Virginia City, he appealed directly to the U.S. Army, stating in a public appeal:

"On the 16th inst., accompanied by the late J. M. Bozeman, I started for Forts C. F. Smith and Phil Kearny. After a day or so of arduous travel, we reached the Yellowstone River and journeyed on it in safety until the 20th inst., when in our noon camp on the Yellowstone, about seven miles this side of Bozeman Ferry, we perceived five Indians approaching us on foot and leading a pony. When within say two hundred and fifty yards I suggested to Mr. Bozeman that we should open fire, to which he made no reply.

"We stood with our rifles ready until the enemy approached to within one hundred yards, at which Bozeman remarked: 'Those are Crows; I know one of them. We will let them come to us and learn where the Sioux and Blackfeet camps are, provided they know.' The Indians meanwhile walked toward us with their hands up, calling, 'Ap-sar-ake' (Crow).

"They shook hands with Mr. B. and proffered the same politeness to me, which I declined by presenting my Henry rifle at them, and at the same moment B. remarked, 'I am fooled; they are Blackfeet. We may, however, get off without trouble.' I then went to our horses (leaving my gun with B.) and had saddled mine, when I saw the chief quickly draw the cover from his fusee, and as I called to B. to shoot, the Indians fired, the ball taking effect in B's right breast, passing completely through him. B. charged on the Indians but did not fire, when another shot took effect in the left breast, and brought poor B. to the ground, a dead man. At that instant I received a bullet through the upper edge of my left shoulder.

"I ran to B. picked up my gun and spoke to him, asking if he was badly hurt. Poor fellow! his last words had been spoken some minutes before I reached the spot: he was 'stone dead.' Finding the Indians pressing me, and my gun not working, I stepped back slowly, trying to fix it, in which I succeeded after retreating say fifty yards. I then opened fire and the first shot brought one of the gentlemen to the sod. I then charged and the other two took to their heels, joining the two that had been saddling B's animal and our pack horse, immediately after B's fall. Having an idea that when collected they might make a rush, I returned to a piece of willow brush, say four hundred yards from the scene of action, giving the Indians a shot or two as I fell back. I remained in the willows about an hour, when I saw the enemy across the river, carrying their dead comrade with them.

"On returning to the camp to examine B, I found but too surely that the poor fellow was out of all earthly trouble. The red men, however, had been in too much of a hurry to scalp him or even take his watch-the latter I brought in. After cutting a pound or so of meat, I started on foot on the back track, swam the Yellowstone, walked thirty miles, and came upon McKenzie and Reshaw's camp, very well satisfied to be so far on the road home and in tolerable safe quarters. The next day I arrived home with a tolerable sore shoulder and pretty well fagged out. A party started out yesterday to bring in B's remains. From what I can glean in the way of information I am satisfied that there is a large party of Blackfeet on the Yellowstone, whose sole object is plunder and scalps.

Yours etc. (Signed) T. W. Coover.

Gallatin Mills, Bozeman, April 22, 1867."[xxxvi]

As luck would have it, there was a preserved native account of the same incident, dictated by a Crow interpreter in 1896:

"In the year 1867 about the last of May or the first of June I was at Fort Laramie in the service of the government, and here the tribe of the Crows were at that time gathered for the purpose of signing a treaty with the government. At this time a war party of young bucks (Crows) set out from the vicinity of Fort C. F. Smith for the purpose of stealing horses from the settlers in the Gallatin Valley. With this party of Crows were five (four) Piegan Indians (one of the largest offshoots of the Blackfoot tribes), renegades from their tribe at that time, among them being Mountain Chief and three sons, one of whom was named Bull.

"Being successful in their raid for horses the band started on their return with about two hundred head of horses and had reached a point six miles below Mission Creek and about sixteen miles east from the present town of Livingston, when they met two white men traveling up the river. One of these was J. M. Bozeman and his companion, I have learned, was T. W. Coover, one of the discovers (sic) of gold in Alder Gulch. Not wishing to harm the whites or to be harmed by them the Crows passed on but the Piegans shortly disappeared from among them which fact was not discovered for some time. The latter not putting in an appearance for some time, the Crows started back to hunt them up and found that they had killed Bozeman while away.

"The Piegans returned to camp with the Crows, but in November returned to the Piegan tribe in northern Montana. Afterwards, during the following years, the three sons of Mountain Chief, together with two other Piegans, set out as a war party for the purpose of stealing horses from their former friends, the Crows. [They] were discovered by a band of Crow warriors under the leading warriors of the Crow tribe, Pretty Eagle and Ball Rock, in the Judith Gap in Judith Basin. [They] intercepted them and killed five of them. They were recognized by the Crows as the sons of Mountain Chief who had just left their camp and who killed Bozeman."[xxxvii]

Of course, accounts recorded decades after the fact did nothing to quell tensions in the present day. A newspaper in Union City, Montana Territory, posted in October of 1867 how Bozeman was murdered by Indians that "were sons of a chief who professes to be at peace with the whites. He does the part of diplomacy, while his sons and followers rob and butcher."[xxxviii] Such tensions between the natives and Americans were not new, obviously, but the local Crow were considered relatively friendly, and the murder of a prominent American often proved a prelude to war.

Rising Tensions

Before the Bozeman Trail gained its name and American travelers, the land originally belonged to the Crows, and it still did afterward according to the 1851 Treaty of Fort Laramie. However, the Crows were not alone on the Plains, and their lands were enticing to other natives. Several other tribes encroached upon the Crow's lands, and by the time the Bozeman Trail earned its name, those tribes had forced them west beyond the Bighorn Rivers.[xxxix]

Among the encroaching tribes, the Sioux were the most persistent, aggressive, and expansionist, allying with other local tribes in their efforts to take the rich Crow lands for themselves. It was this alliance that forced back the Crow.[xl]

By 1864, the Crow had other encroachers on their lands as well. With additional pressure from the Blackfeet, the Crows found themselves at the edges of the buffalo lands, bordered by hostile tribes and facing American settlers and prospectors traveling through their richest game areas. The whites, at least, were just passing through, and that, along with their mutual enemies (the Blackfeet and Sioux), meant that, if not an alliance, then at least the two groups could form a détente of sorts.[xli]

The Crows did not accept whites blindly, though. Fur traders, long accustomed to dealing with natives and considered by some whites to be effectively native themselves, were welcome within Crow lands. Settlers and especially prospectors were not, and even on the brink of losing their lands, the Crow assaulted prospectors in 1863, killing one of them.[xlii] In general, though, before the Bozeman Trail, as long as the whites passed through Crow lands quickly, they were left alone.[xliii] Even after the Bozeman Trail's creation, the Crows did not initially react, mainly because the majority of the Trail crossed through lands taken by other tribes.[xliv]

However, the new residents of the Powder River Country, the Sioux, did not take kindly to whites traversing their new real estate. As early as 1864, travelers were advised not to traverse the Bozeman Trail except in very large wagon trains.[xlv] The U.S. Army also suffered; that year, a Captain Townshend and several soldiers set out along the Trail with a wagon train. The Sioux attacked his train, killing four of his soldiers in the assault.[xlvi]

In response to Sioux raids along the Trail, the United States Army closed the Trail in 1865 to mount the Powder River Expedition against the Sioux alliance that kept ravaging settlers and the beleaguered Crows. With the Civil War nearing its end, spare men were hard to come by, but still the Powder River Expedition prepared, commanded by Brigadier General Patrick Connor.[xlvii]

Connor

Charged with keeping the roads and trails of the plains open, Connor's expedition was war in all but name. Underequipped, and without enough men, the Expedition turned out to be little more than a series of limited skirmishes, fortification construction, and requisitions for more men and materiel.[xlviii]

Given three divisions to complete his task, General Connor made the best of the situation. Each division was given a region under their control in order to better operate over the vast stretches of the Plains.[xlix] The eastern, or right division, with Colonel Nelson Cole commanding, was charged with marching from Omaha, Nebraska along the north end of the Black Hills through the northern boundaries of the Trail, linking up with Connor and the middle division.[l] The middle division, with Colonel Samuel Walker commanding, would march from Fort Laramie to the Black Hills, linking up with the eastern division before joining with General Connor.[li] The western, or left division, under the direct command of General Connor, would march along the length of the Bozeman Trail itself, at the end of which the general expected to link his three divisions together.[lii]

Almost from the start, the Expedition faced trouble. The various division commanders had a foggy notion of which parts of the Powder River Country they were to march through, with the varied surveys of the region not helping. The biggest problem, however, was the soldiers' refusal to march.[liii] Occurring at the climax of the American Civil War, the Expedition's soldiers expected to be discharged and allowed to return to their homes, not stuck in the middle of nowhere fighting another battle. Dissuaded from mutiny with the helpful aid of artillery, the various divisions finally got under way in July. [liv]

The Expedition faced vast open country, and that, coupled with lack of supplies, logistics, and communication beyond runners and scouts, quickly took their toll. Men succumbed to scurvy, and the east and middle divisions failed to link up on schedule, thanks largely to the lack of proper surveys of the region and general lack of knowledge of the terrain.[lv] This lack of knowledge resulted in supply failures, further exacerbating the Expedition's plight.

With the soldiers lacking food in a region sparse of forage for anything except oxen and birds, the natives pounced, attacking the separated divisions. The natives' attacks were a rude awakening for the soldiers, as among the three divisions only the Indian scouts had knowledge of the area or experience fighting in the West. Expecting nearly nude savages flinging spears and arrows, the natives' use of rifles and captured Army uniforms took them completely by surprise.[lvi] Despite the lack of supplies and the Indian raids, the middle and east divisions managed to link up in early September, but as the united divisions marched onward to join with General Connor's division, 225 horses and mules died from heat exhaustion, starvation, or cold thanks to a recent mountain storm.[lvii]

With the loss of pack animals, the soldiers had no choice but to burn excess equipment, lest it fall into the hands of the natives. However, before the soldiers could dispose of the extra equipment, the natives, clad in American uniforms, attacked. After repelling the natives, the soldiers proceeded to burn or bury whatever they could not take with them.[lviii] By the middle of September, the divisions, working off 60 days' worth of rations after traveling for 82 days, most of them barefoot, faced continued assaults from the natives as they marched almost in desperation to complete their missions.[lix]

Traveling across 1,200 in terrain barely crossed by white men, the Expedition would've at least succeeded in performing a great surveying of the region, if a surveyor had been present. Poorly prepared, planned, coordinated, or executed, the forces finally concluded their duty at Fort Laramie in early October, both divisions doubling back to avoid annihilation.[lx] The great "success" of the Expedition consisted of the surveys for the construction of three forts planned to bolster the defense of the Bozeman Trail. In the end, these forts would only prove to exacerbate tensions.

Both the natives' view of the expedition and General Connor's offer an idea of the end result. "The Indians, thinking that the commander had voluntarily retired from their front, again hastened to the road, passing General Connor's retiring column to the east of his line of march, and again commenced their devilish work of pillage, plunder and massacre."[lxi]

General Connor himself is reported to have stated in regard to the Expedition, "You have doubtless noticed the singular termination of the late campaign against the Indians. The truth is, rather harm than good was done, and our troops were, in one sense, driven out of their country by the Indians. I am more solicitous for the honor of the service than I am for my own. I do not feel sore over the treatment accorded me, but think the policy of the government toward the Indians mistaken and very unjust to the Western people."[lxii]

Declared a resounding success, the Bozeman Trail reopened in 1866.

Though the Sioux preyed on travelers along the Bozeman Trail across their new domain, as mentioned earlier, the lands were still recognized by the 1851 Treaty as Crow territory, and initially the influx of traders benefited the Crow. As a natural consequence of the antiquated treaty, loss of Crow land, and the rising power of the hostile Sioux, the federal government gathered leaders from the local tribes in an effort to ratify a new treaty.[lxiii] Recognizing how far west the Crow now resided, they were not invited to the negotiation table for the new treaty.[lxiv]

At the same time, the Army continued fortifying the three new forts in the region: Fort Reno, Fort Phil Kearny, and Fort C. F. Smith.[lxv] Fort Reno, originally named Fort Connor after the Expedition's commander, began construction on August 14, 1865. An officer at the fort's creation wrote in his diary, "The Powder River is, at this point, a very rapid stream, water muddy, like the Missouri; timber very plenty, ranging back from the river from one-half to a mile; grass not very good; no chance to cut any hay anywhere on the river."[lxvi]

A 19ᵗʰ century depiction of Fort Reno

In June 1866, Colonel Henry B. Carrington surveyed the area to see if he could find a better place for a fort. Finding none, he set to work bolstering the fortification, renaming it Fort Reno.[lxvii] The first fort along the Trail after Fort Laramie, this fort's role in the coming years would remain marginal, serving as a vital if unremarkable gatekeeper for the Trail's entrance.[lxviii]

Carrington

Fort C. F. Smith, placed roughly halfway along the Trail, would have a much greater role. Established on August 12, 1866 under the orders of Colonel Carrington, the fort found itself far removed from any other civilization.

Fort Phil Kearny lay 91 miles to the east, and Virginia City nearly 300 miles to the west. The fort's complement faced a vast, open landscape that the fort fortunately provided a very good view to observe.[lxix]

An early sign of how stretched and isolated the Army was in the region is indicated in a report from someone who resided at both Forts Reno and Fort Phil Kearny. According to this resident,

"From the day I landed at Reno and Phil Kearny, Fort C. F. Smith was an unknown quantity. From February 20, 1867, until April 26, 1868, not a word came from there except once, when a party of Crows came to our fort, about forty of them, with pelts and skins to trade. The Indians reported all quiet at Fort C. F. Smith."[lxx]

As the previous quote foreshadows, Fort C.F. Smith would play a vital role in the later story of the Bozeman Trail. It was Fort Phil Kearny, however, that drew the ire of the natives and precipitated the looming conflict. Built under the direction of Colonel Carrington, Fort Phil Kearny's construction began July 15, 1866. The largest, most heavily garrisoned of the three new forts, it stood as a monument to the might of the Army and their intentions to defend the Bozeman Trail and the Plains in general from native assault.[lxxi]

G. Coudert's picture of Fort Phil Kearny

The fort was strategically located near the Piney River, where forage grass, fresh water, and timber lay aplenty, and its strategic location also rendered it a grave insult to the natives, for it rested in the heart of a rich gaming area.[lxxii] Fort Phil Kearny earned the nickname "the hated post on the Little Piney," and it would play a prominent role in the looming conflict.[lxxiii]

The Start of Red Cloud's War

Red Cloud did not just appear onto the scene to crusade for his people's lands and way of life. Dubbed at the time the "Red Napoleon of the Plains," Red Cloud rose as a prominent war chief of the Ogalala Sioux thanks to his prowess as a warrior.[lxxiv] An impressive skirmisher, his skills earned him a following with the young warriors, but his true prominence would come when the Bozeman Trail gouged its way through the heart of the buffalo range.[lxxv]

Red Cloud

Had it not been for a disastrous example of bad timing on the part of the Army, what was to be known to many Americans as Red Cloud's War might have been averted. In fact, it was not until after 1862, when Union Pacific Railroad worker began surveying a route through the southern buffalo hunting grounds, that trouble arose. The Native Americans relied on summer buffalo hunts and feared that the railroad running directly through their southern hunting grounds would disrupt the annual hunt. Numerous Plains people of many different tribes met at these southern hunting camps during the annual summer hunt, and despite current animosities they met together to celebrate feasts and to hold joint councils. Increasingly, these councils were concerned with their common enemy, and intertribal rivalries were put aside.

While the Army negotiated for safe passage across the Bozeman Trail, they were simultaneously building forts and importing detachments of soldiers to heighten protection for settlers. Furthermore, in the few periods when Red Cloud was of a mind to join negotiations, some off-putting examples of American might appeared at the most inopportune time.

For example, in the winter of 1865, General William Tecumseh Sherman, of Civil War fame, visited the winter headquarters of Colonel Carrington in order to "review"[1] the officer's suitability for relocation to Powder River with his contingent of troops. Only a few months earlier, Carrington had worked as an army surveyor, helping to prepare the Platte River region for the railroad. When he arrived in Laramie commanding a unit of 700 soldiers from the 2nd Battalion and the 18th Infantry, Red Cloud cut short his participation in the council. Not only did Carrington's intimidating arrival constitute a "stunningly ill-timed move,"[2] but his caravan was filled with supplies for building and equipping a series of forts, complete with household items for officers' families. Red Cloud stormed out in a fury, complaining that the federal government

[1] History.com

[2] Donald McCaig, The Bozeman Trail, *Smithsonian Magazine*, September 30, 2000 – www.smithsonianmag.com/travel/the-bozeman-trail-68326894

was forcing its way across the Montana pass while requesting permission to occupy it at the same time. He subsequently declared he would not participate in subsequent councils.

Sherman

The Connecticut-born Colonel Carrington was largely oblivious to his unfortunate time of arrival. Under orders from Major General John Pope, the 42-year-old colonel with no combat experience in the Civil War was instructed to design, build, and staff several forts along the Bozeman Trail. Carrington was described by one historian as an "ardent anti-slavery man"[3] whose pre-military years were spent practicing law in Ohio, with an expertise in engineering and design. He was physically diminutive and sported long hair with a dark beard, and the Indians took to calling him Little White Chief. By the time of his departure from Fort Laramie, Carrington had brought almost 2,000 new recruits with him, plus a force of 300 Civil War veterans to help occupy the forts. With these men, Carrington ably staffed Fort Sedgewick, Salt Lake City, and Fort Bridger, and on August 12, 1866, he began construction of Fort C.F. Smith, 70 miles to the northwest. However, the remaining force with which to man Fort Phil Kearny and the proposed wagon route around the Big Horn Mountains was only comprised of the 2nd Battalion of eight companies, barely suitable for sustaining even peacetime operations.

Perhaps more than the show of force witnessed in Fort Laramie with Carrington's arrival, the presence of 12 women, 11 children, and a host of domestic items that included mowing machines

---

[3] Dee Brown, *The Fetterman Massacre*, Integrated Media, Open Road, New York, October 23, 2012

delivered the final insult to Red Cloud. By the time Carrington departed Laramie in the early summer, several Indians not allied with Red Cloud warned him about the likelihood of hostile actions against his company and the projected forts.

Entirely without experience in fighting on the frontier, Carrington remained optimistic, escorting 226 wagons further into the Powder River country. Many of the horses and supplies intended for his use went missing before his departure, but Carrington continued to fulfill his assignment on schedule. He stopped first at the already established Fort Reno, nearly 180 miles south of Laramie, and left a garrison there for its protection. Continuing up the Bozeman Trail for over 60 miles, he selected a suitable spot for the construction of a large fort, which he designed and oversaw through the entire process. The infamous enclosure was soon named Fort Phil Kearny after Major General Phillip Kearney, who died at the Battle of Chantilly a few days after Second Bull Run.

Although Indian actions were directed against nearly all travelers and forts along the Bozeman Trail, Red Cloud, who refused to sign a non-aggression treaty, chose Fort Phil Kearny and Henry Carrington as the primary objects of his attacks. The raids, usually involving a small number of warriors, began from the first day of the fort's construction, and were often focused on teams of woodcutters and arriving supply wagons.

Initially, Red Cloud refused to attend negotiations regarding the Bozeman Trail. A later invitation for negotiations swayed Red Cloud, and he made the trek to Fort Laramie to once more decry the Trail. Also present at the table was Colonel Carrington, preparing the Army to hold the Trail against native assault. Rising to his feet and in opposition to the more favorable attitudes of less notable chiefs, Red Cloud pointed right at the Colonel and declared, "You are the white eagle who has come to steal the road. The Great Father sends us presents, and wants us to sell him the road, but the white chief comes with soldiers to steal it, before the Indian says yes or no! I will talk with you no more. I and my people will go now, and we will fight you! As long as I live, I will fight for the last hunting grounds of my people!"[lxxvi] Thus declared, Red Cloud drew his blanket around him and left in disgust.[lxxvii]

To the U.S. Army, Red Cloud's leadership of the war against the Bozeman Trail was apparent, but locating him was difficult. In the numerous raids leading up to the Fetterman Massacre, American scouts could not affirm that Red Cloud was present, or whether he was leading from a safe distance. Regardless, his mark on the resistance to American use of the Bozeman Trail was unmistakable. On July 17, 1866, the Cazeau train attempted passage from Fort Collins. Peter Cazeau and Henry Arrison led the two wagons, with three postal employees, Cazeau's Oglala wife Mary, and four children. Camping at Peno Creek, only six miles from Fort Phil Kearny, Cazeau's group was approached by a small band of Northern Cheyenne coming from a council with officers at the fort. Demonstrating no aggression, they tarried at the camp, but they were soon joined by a band of Sioux, demanding that the Cheyenne fight with them in a raid against the fort. The Cheyenne refused and were berated as cowards before eventually being driven from the camp. The incident seemed to have passed, but the Sioux returned the following morning and killed Cazeau, Arrison, and the three employees. Arrison's wife hid in the brush with the children, and they were later rescued by soldiers from the fort.

Three days after the Cazeau massacre, another small wagon train was attacked by an alliance of Sioux and Cheyenne at Crazy Woman Creek, a fork of the Powder River. Unlike the Cazeau train, the Crazy Woman Creek attack was defended by a unit of 20 soldiers on their way to Phil Kearney. Lieutenants Daniels and Templeton scouted ahead and were attacked by a band of 50. Daniels was killed, and Templeton escaped with an arrow in his back and severe facial wounds.

He was able to reach the train, and the wagons were immediately circled. The whites settled in for a day-long battle, and they were eventually rescued by the arrival of a larger train offering reinforcements.

By 1866, traffic across the Bozeman Trail had slowed to a trickle due to Red Cloud's efforts. The U.S. Army had no answer to the war chief's "textbook guerilla war,"[4] successfully accomplished in large part through the efforts of Crazy Horse and other young leaders of the Sioux, Cheyenne, and Arapaho. Crazy Horse, like Red Cloud, was born in the central Plains, near present-day Rapid City, South Dakota. Brought up around the white man's environment, he was nicknamed "Curly" as a young boy. However, by the time he reached maturity, the future leader of the Oglala Sioux was hailed as an "able tactician and determined warrior."[5] The son of an Oglala medicine man, Crazy Horse later related a vision from his youth declaring that he would distinguish himself as a warrior against the invading whites.

As an expert in erecting strong structures for defense, Carrington had done well in selecting a location for Fort Phil Kearny, but the situation was still far from perfect. The largest and, in a tactical sense, most important facility in north central Wyoming, it was built on good ground between the Big and Little Piney Creeks to the east of present-day Story, Wyoming, with dimensions of 800 by 600 feet. The fort's defenders had a good field of fire in every direction, and good access to water. However, it was not built on the area's highest ground, and was easily observable by its enemies. Carrington's logic was likely caught in a dilemma of choosing higher ground, but losing access to resources. Similarly, the nearest available stands of wood were located several miles away, and every woodcutting unit venturing out came under attack on an almost daily basis. Since the mid-summer of 1866 into the winter months, Fort Phil Kearny withstood 50 skirmishes with Indian raiding parties, which devised various ambushes for anyone leaving the fort. This regimen continued over a two-year period, as the guerilla war of Red Cloud and Crazy Horse laid siege to a generally defensive-minded American army.

While raids continued against local travelers, both sides prepared their respective forces for conflict, in the process placing the beleaguered Crow between a rock and a hard place. With their old enemy the Sioux on the warpath, the village elders received a surprise when several Sioux chiefs visited the Crow to establish an alliance against the American soldiers.[lxxviii] While younger men amongst the Crow favored an alliance, the older Crow, their long memories of the Sioux as enemies intact, decided for the time to a tepid lack of commitment.[lxxix]

The old animosities with the Sioux lingering in their minds, and with hopes of reclaiming the Powder River Country in their hearts, the Crow went to the Army to discuss an alliance against the Sioux and their allies in late August of 1866 at Fort C. F. Smith.[lxxx] Through an interpreter, the Crow warned the Army of a large band of Sioux gathering for war, and also reminded the Army of a treaty the Crow signed at Fort Benton promising them a reservation where they could farm and trade.[lxxxi] The American response was noncommittal overall but intimated support for the Crow against the Sioux. Given papers and rations, the fort's commander, Captain Nathaniel C. Kinney, allowed the Crow to trade with the fort's resident sutlers.[lxxxii]

It did not take long for the Army to learn of the dissension amongst the Crow between the young and the old, who wished to remain friends with the US government. For many older Crow, the Army was their best chance to regain their old lands now dominated by the Sioux, the lands now crossed by the Bozeman Trail.[lxxxiii]

The Trail now rose as a sticking point between Crow and American relations, as the loss of

[4] Exploring Off the Beaten Path.com, Fetterman Massacre – www.exploringoffthebeatenpath.com/Battlefields/Fetterman/Massacre/index.html
[5] Encyclopaedia Britannica, Crazy Horse, Sioux Chief – www.britannica.com/biography/Crazy-Horse#ref150798

game along the route from travelers offset the benefits of trade. Furthermore, despite American insistence to the contrary, many Crow felt the Trail's existence lacked proper authority, having been blazed, named, and now used without the Crow's permission.[lxxxiv]

With less than a thousand soldiers and a trail spanning over 600 miles across land best described as "the middle of nowhere," Carrington faced a daunting theater of war against an enemy that knew the land like the back of their hand.[lxxxv] Unable to defend a Trail that most people had the good sense not to use anyway, maintaining friendly relations with the Crow and continued support against the Sioux took priority in the war.[lxxxvi] A lieutenant by the name of George M. Templeton remarked in his journal following a council with the Crow on Halloween of 1866, "[F]rom all I can see I am of the impression that if the government does not take decided measures very soon in regards to the Sioux, that the Crows will enter a league and for the first time make war with the whites."[lxxxvii] As he saw it, the lack of troops was the main issue, not only for the Army to commence effective operations in the war, but also to protect and bolster the Crow and maintain their friendship.[lxxxviii]

While both sides courted the Crow as allies, the war continued. In the summer of 1866, another wagon train braved the Sioux infested Bozeman Trail, its tale repeated countless times across the Plains. Reaching Fort Laramie, the train grouped together with other, smaller trains and a cattle drive to bolster their numbers before moving on across the Trail to their respective destinations.[lxxxix] "The train moved on without serious incident. The country was alive with Indians. There were signs of fighting- burned wagons and dead stock in places, and at times the Story outfit would spy on Indians at a distance. But it was not until within about ten miles of Fort Reno that there was any open hostility toward the train."[xc]

As the whites neared the presumed safety of one of the Trail's forts, the natives finally made their move, unleashing a hail of arrows and stealing the cattle though they were later recaptured.[xci] Though there were no deaths, the train was forced to stop at Fort Phil Kearny, then still under construction, and the small complement of soldiers was unable to leave the fort to protect the wagon train or even finish building the fort. Halted three miles from the fort to preserve the area's forage for military use, the traveler noted the distance was too far to aid the train if the natives attacked.[xcii]

Forced to wait and surrounded by Indians, the train decided to take matters into their own hands. Under cover of night, the train advanced, and in the process discovered that the natives, finding the settler's repeating Remington rifles far more intimidating than the single shot Springfield rifles of the soldiers, gave them a wide berth.[xciii] Attacked at night with no loss of life, and with the natives repelled each time, the wagon train waited out daylight and made sure only to travel after sundown.

Eventually, the wagon train managed to reach Fort C. F. Smith and the surrounding Crow, who at this early point in the war found neutrality better than picking a side, as the Sioux left them alone to focus on the Army and the local game returned thanks to fewer travelers.[xciv] From Fort C. F. Smith, the wagon train continued to Virginia City without incident.[xcv]

While this wagon train traveled, the first major battle of the war occurred, and it was an embarrassing loss for the Army that proved how under-equipped, under-manned, and under-estimating of their native foes they truly were. In fact, it would be the worst defeat the Army suffered against Native Americans until the Battle of the Little Bighorn.

The Fetterman Massacre

"Look at me - I am poor and naked, but I am the chief of the nation. We do not want riches, but we want to train our children right. Riches will do us no good. We could not take them with us to the other world. We do not want riches. We want peace and love." – Red Cloud

The first good news for the officers who wanted a more offensive-oriented policy finally came in November 1866, in the form of Lieutenant Horatio S. Bingham's Company C of the 2nd Cavalry as reinforcements. With Bingham came two infantry captains, James Powell and William J. Fetterman. Of one mind with the officers already serving at the fort, Fetterman's nature was to speak out where others would not. While every officer wanted to undertake an offensive against Red Cloud and his guerilla raids, it was Fetterman who pushed for the extermination of all indigenous men of fighting age throughout the Powder River region, including the Bozeman Trail. Despite Carrington holding the superior rank, Fetterman was aware of General Cooke's orders, and that Cooke had threatened Carrington with a court-martial due to missing reports that were later found to have been delayed in the postal system. Moreover, among the new officers, it was Fetterman who held the highest rank in a technical sense, since he was breveted as a colonel. By dint of that promotion, he could exercise most prerogatives of a colonel, albeit subsisting on the pay of a captain. Likely born in New London, Connecticut, Fetterman was the son of a career officer of Pennsylvania German ancestry. Five years before his posting at Fort Phil Kearny, Fetterman enlisted with the Delaware Infantry and had received his brevet rank for gallant conduct.

Fetterman was a colorful character, but reckless to some, and historians still debate the merits of his actions while at Fort Phil Kearny. For decades, biographers and historians maintained that it was Fetterman's foolishness and brash disobedience of orders that led to the ensuing massacre that now bears his name. Regardless, to say that he was "critical of Carrington's defensive posture"[6] must be taken as a gross understatement. Fetterman was openly scornful of Carrington, both in and out of his presence, despite his own lack of fighting experience on the frontier against Plains Indians. In his correspondence, there was no veiling of his sentiments. A November letter to Charles Terry, one which was later published in *The Annals of Wyoming*, he stated unequivocally, "We are afflicted with an incompetent commanding officer."[7] He added optimistically that the general belief among the officers held that Fort Phil Kearny would be "relieved of him in the coming reorganization, he going to the 18th, and we becoming the 27th Infantry."[8]

Throughout November 1866, Red Cloud raised the intensity of his raids as Fetterman continued to express contempt for Carrington and his tactics. In a search for any maneuver that might "tempt, provoke, or enrage,"[9] raiding parties were surprised to see how susceptible Army troops were to pursuing decoys into ambush situations. Taunts and gestures by a few warriors approaching either the fort or woodcutter trains were often enough to draw the desired response. Groups of women in sight of the fort mocked officers already laboring under an unaccustomed restraint imposed by their commander. However, the most effective maneuver involved small parties appearing to confront troops before suddenly fleeing as a tactical feint. Such simplistic staging appealed directly to the Americans' misperception of possessing the upper hand, a failing which would result in repeated heartaches for the troops.

Red Cloud's warriors played the ruse well, where the army did not. In mid-November, Fetterman received permission from Carrington to prepare his own ambush and draw a sizeable

---

[6] Colonel Henry B. Carrington, Margaret I. Carrington, *The Fetterman Massacre; and the Official Reports*, Ed. Ann & Harry, 7th Edition, U.S. Government, Washington, D.C., 1888-1890

[7] 3rd 1000, The Fetterman Massacre

[8] 3rd 1000, The Fetterman Massacre

[9] Exploring Off the Beaten Path

number of the enemy into firing range of what was intended to be a superior force. In one of many such underestimations, Fetterman was surprised to see the enemy sniff out the trap and make off with a bunch of Army cattle to the opposite bank of the Powder River.

The stakes were raised again in early December. Crazy Horse and Red Cloud reasoned that if decoy tactics were so effective against woodcutter patrols, they may serve equally well against larger forces. Joining in the plans for a raid on December 6 was Little Wolf, who had counseled peace and signed the Laramie agreement. However, he was irreconcilable over the massacre at Sand Creek, and thus bent on retribution. Black Shield and White Bull shared the sentiment, supporting the increased scope of future raids.

On the morning of December 6, a wood train was attacked, as it had been repeatedly since the Army's arrival, and Carrington's lookout tower, built on nearby Pilot Hill, was effective in alerting the fort to danger. A detail of 30 cavalrymen was sent out to relieve the woodcutters under the command of Fetterman and Lieutenant Bingham.

To that point, the scenario was much like every other day at Fort Phil Kearny. However, in an unusual display of forthrightness, Carrington himself led a force of 25 mounted infantry out of the fort with Lieutenant George Grummond as his second-in-command. Carrington planned to have Fetterman drive the attacking decoys away from the wood train and toward the infantrymen circling around Lodge Trail Ridge, where the retreating enemy would be cut off.

All went well in the beginning. Fetterman reached the wood train in short order and sent the attackers retreating toward the location where Fetterman believed Carrington to be. However, Carrington and Grummond had not yet arrived at the appointed spot. The second sign of trouble appeared when Bingham's cavalry became dangerously strung out, isolating the men, many of whom were inexperienced. A general panic arose within the cavalry as the fleeing Indians inexplicably turned on them, now able to attack soldiers individually, as they were too far from immediate support. To complicate matters, Bingham himself suddenly galloped off in a different direction for an unknown reason, leaving his confounded men behind. One theory claims that he was going to the rear lines to rally the troops, but the more likely scenario suggests that he set off in pursuit of a small group of Indian decoys. Regardless, he was soon cut off from his own men, and from Fetterman's force. Unable to fight his way back, Bingham was felled by a barrage of arrows.

G. Coudert's picture of Pilot Hill from Fort Kearny

The next misstep in a series of misfortunes for the troops saw Carrington become unexpectedly engaged in a separate skirmish to the north of Lodge Trail Ridge. He was able to weather the attack and eventually meet up with Fetterman on the Bozeman Trail in the Peno Valley. Grummond had made the same serious error as Bingham by going his own way and finding himself cut off after pursuing a phantom force. He was fortunate to find his way back to Carrington by hacking through a large force with his saber.

Once reunited with their commanding officer, the collective found its way back to the fort. They considered themselves fortunate to have lost only Bingham and two sergeants, with four soldiers wounded. The Indians suffered 10 dead.

Red Cloud's forces were not discouraged at the failure to inflict greater damage on the opposing forces. Now operating under the assumption that pursuing decoys represented an allure the American cavalrymen were unable to resist, they resolved to continue the tactic at regular intervals. For Crazy Horse and other chiefs, a belief emerged that the strategy might work against the fort itself. Carrington, with no battle experience in either the Civil War or frontier fighting, was likely rattled by the daily anxiety and suspense. However, he probably saw the larger picture better than his subordinate officers, and he issued orders prohibiting anyone from pursuing the enemy over Lost Trail Ridge, for any reason. That order was tested less than two weeks later when the wood train was again attacked on December 19. The relief force was sent out under the command of Captain Powell, who followed Carrington's order to the letter. The attacking decoys were driven off, but no subsequent pursuit was offered. Once again, the Sioux alliance shrugged off the result and prepared another decoy attack in a few days.

The next raid occurred on December 21, which saw Crazy Horse and his fellow chiefs employ the same tactic as seen in all the previous raids. Red Cloud recalled in hindsight that he had consulted a tribal hermaphrodite said to possess special powers before the battle. As Red Cloud stood on the butte overlooking the projected battlefield, the "half man"[10] rode his pony in a "crazed manner"[11] in four separate maneuvers, between the butte and Lodge Trail Ridge. Following each pattern, he drew his hands to his face, palms upward, before continuing. He explained to Red Cloud that with each drawing of his hands, he was scooping up the lives of U.S. Army soldiers, and following the final repetition, he claimed that 100 blue-clad soldiers would be killed on that day.

On the morning of December 21, nearly 2,000 warriors concealed themselves along the road to the north of Fort Phil Kearny as the wood train left the fort for the pine stands at approximately 10:00 am. The attack by the Indian decoys commenced an hour later, involving only a small band of warriors. As he had two days earlier, Carrington gave command of the relief party to Captain Powell.

What happened at this point is still a subject of debate, aside from the fact that Brevet Colonel Fetterman eventually led the rescue unit out of the fort. It is suggested by many that Fetterman "pulled rank" on Powell, but either way, there's no doubt Fetterman was displeased by Powell's willingness to obey the non-pursuit order. Equally clear was that Fetterman wanted an immediate fight to end the conflict once and for all. He was already a notable figure at Fort Phil Kearny for an extraordinary boast he made before the entire company: "With 80 men, I could ride through the whole Sioux nation."[12]

Though the declaration is historically supported in one form or another, some disagreement ensued between various officers and enlisted men long after the fact. According to Private F.M. Fessenden, Carrington never made an offer of command to Captain Powell, and Fetterman simply asked for the assignment. Even the order of non-pursuit as an ironclad directive was disputed by some of the men present. Fessenden added that no one substantiated the order, least of all on December 21. All that was heard among the foot soldiers and mounted infantry was a simple order by Carrington: "Colonel, go out and bring in that wood train."[13] In addition to the first decoys, Crazy Horse and 10 warriors rode into view of the fort, at close range. Carrington fired a round of artillery at them, and they feigned running away.

Accounts of subsequent actions taken by Fetterman are wildly disparate. One version claims that he did not proceed directly to the wood train, and with Indian decoys already fleeing, he intended to cut them off. In seeing that the woodcutters were safe for the time being, Fetterman's only purpose in continuing, according to this account, was to execute a punitive action, and he chose the group led by Crazy Horse.

In terms of any orders for restraint, there was likely no deterrent coming from his fellow officers. Lieutenant Grummond, with a long history of discipline problems, and Captain Frederick Brown, who declined a transfer east so that he could personally participate in the Bozeman Trail conflict, served as Fetterman's immediate subordinates. Grummond, despite nearly being killed in an earlier raid, had a new bride at the fort, but he seemed more eager than ever to kill as many Sioux and Cheyenne as he could. Brown staked his entire military future on "tak[ing] care of Red Cloud personally"[14] before going on to any other assignment.

[10] WikiVisually, Fetterman Fight – www.wikivisually.com/wiki/Fetterman_Massacre

[11] WikiVisually

[12] Exploring Off the Beaten Path

[13] Shannon Smith Calitri, Give Me Eighty Men: Shattering the Myth of the Fetterman Massacre, Free Republic – www.freerepublic.com/focus/f-vetscor/1638957/posts

[14] 3rd 1000, The Fetterman Massacre

A second variation of the events theorizes that Fetterman did proceed directly to rescue the woodcutters, reaching them by noon. However, upon being assured that they were no longer in danger, he veered suddenly to the east on the Bozeman Trail, then north up the Lodge Trail Ridge, very near the imaginary line drawn by Carrington. With him came the 80 men to which he had referred in his famous boast, plus one. Ensuing military analysis generally points to Fetterman's wisdom of seizing the initiative as he pursued the band of approximately 40 Indians executing the raid. No one in the fort felt the slightest alarm upon hearing gunfire along the top of the ridge. Fetterman's force was the largest ever sent out, and no one had ever seen more than 100 warriors gathered in the region before. All army personnel proceeded on the assumption that this day would be no different.

According to eyewitness accounts from the fort, Fetterman was out of sight within minutes. Unaware of the large number of enemy warriors waiting over the ridge, and with the unusually sizeable force under Fetterman, Carrington likely assumed that he had sent enough firepower to protect the woodcutters and drive out the raiding party. Needless to say, Carrington was underinformed. Frontiersman Jim Bridger, who as a rule avoided the region altogether while trading, had counted up to 500 lodges encamped at the Tongue River. Although such a number did not represent the entire force of the Indian alliance, most of the Minneconjou Sioux and Northern Cheyenne arrived at the encampment behind Lodge Trail Ride on the previous night. Based on the Army's previous experiences, 50-100 would cover the retreat of the decoys leading soldiers farther over the ridge, where they would meet a body of no more than 100 warriors, as in previous raids. Given that assumption, from a tactician's standpoint, Fetterman's action was not entirely irrational. Technically, however, when Fetterman crossed the ridge, he was clearly in violation of his orders, if such orders to avoid pursuit at a certain distance were actually given.

Debate continues over the precise time at which Lieutenant Grummond left the fort in support of Fetterman. One account suggests that he rode out in advance, but another suggests that he left two hours later after attempting to round up the mounts necessary for all the men. Grummond's men were armed with seven-shot Spencer carbines, an important support for infantrymen carrying one-shot muzzle-loader rifles. Two civilian scouts, James Wheatley and Isaac Fisher, went out with Grummond, armed with Henry 16-shot lever action rifles. Upon Grummond's departure, one account claims that Carrington told him to "remind"[15] Fetterman not to pursue over the ridge, but other men present at the fort that day doubted such an order was given.

When the decoys disappeared over the ridge, it was likely Grummond, not Fetterman, who set off in hot pursuit, since he led the mounted soldiers. As he encountered a massive number of Lakota waiting for him on the other side, another group of Indians raced up the side of the ridge to seal off his retreat. What ensued was a massive attack of proportions never seen in battle against the Plains Indians, with over 40,000 arrows shot over a period of 30-45 minutes.

Fetterman, unable to keep up with Grummond's cavalry, struggled to reach an outcropping of rocks to employ as a natural shelter. This locale later came to be known as Infantry Hill. With Fetterman entirely cut off, Grummond attempted to reach him by racing along the top of the ridge and fighting through the enemy's rear guard that sealed off his retreat. A few cavalrymen were able to reach Fetterman, but most did not, and Grummond was likely among the first killed. In a hail of arrows, along with some bullets, Grummond fell, swinging his infamous saber. Wheatley and Fisher, civilian scouts, found a fold in the ridge in which to hide, and they attempted to provide cover for the retreating cavalry. However, even with their superior arms, they were soon overwhelmed and killed. The shrinking Indian circle around Fetterman's position

---

[15] Exploring Off the Beaten Path

grew so small that some warriors were wounded by their own across the way.

Once the scouts and cavalry were neutralized, the entire Indian force turned its full attention on Fetterman and the small band of infantry still alive in the rocks. The remaining soldiers surely knew what was about to befall them, and before long, everyone in the fort knew as well. Cavalrymen reaching Infantry Hill cut loose their mounts, all of which ran at once back to the fort in a chilling scene.

How each man in the infantry died is largely unknown, as only Sioux, Cheyenne, and Arapaho warriors were numbered among the survivors. Within the approximated time frame of the event, a combination of cold winter weather and the limited muzzle-loader rifles indicate that the battle became a hand-to-hand conflict within minutes. One theory holds that Fetterman and Brown committed suicide together, each with a pistol to the other's head. Their bodies were found next to one another, and both allegedly had powder burns on their faces. Other accounts suggest that Brown shot himself, but that remains uncorroborated. Such assumptions speak to the anticipated tortures of a brief and grotesque captivity on the part of the soldiers. The claim of American Horse, later a great Oglala Lakota chief, that he personally killed Fetterman with his war club before slashing him, may well be accurate. The state of Fetterman's body backed up the warrior's story.

A picture of the hill where Fetterman and his men were slaughtered

A plaque at the site of the massacre

Among the last of Fetterman's unit to die was Company Bugler, John Metzger, who used his instrument as a weapon to the last. For showing such courage in the face of his enemies, Metzger's body was not mutilated in any way, and he was covered with a buffalo robe. His bugle is on display to the present-day at the Jim Gatchell Museum in Buffalo, Wyoming.

For its part, the alliance of Red Cloud and Crazy Horse, Black Shield and White Bull, the Cheyenne lost only two men, the Arapaho one, and the Lakota Sioux 60. Some of the Native American casualties were the result of friendly fire.

The *Annals of Wyoming* described the brief battle as occurring somewhat differently. Fetterman is listed as having been stabbed more than slashed, and the soldiers are said to have held out for 40 minutes. Much description is given to the mutilation of soldiers' bodies, as a way of preventing them from using their senses to experience happiness in the spirit world. Carrington made a detailed list describing a "litany"[16] of stunning atrocities. These included "eyes torn out, laid on rocks, noses cut off, ears cut off, arms taken from sockets, private parts severed and independently placed on the person."[17] The Indians were in possession of a few guns, but only six of the 81 soldiers were shot.

When the distant sounds of battle died away at the fort, Carrington sent out another detail under the command of Ten Eyck with instructions to support Fetterman in any way he could. Those at the fort waited tensely for news of the day's events, as did the families of Indian attackers far to the rear. Famed medicine man and holy man Black Elk remembered in his later

[16] Encyclopedia Virginia, Fetterman Massacre – www.encyclopediavirginia.org/media_player?mets_filename=evm00002737mets.html

[17] Encyclopedia Virginia, Fetterman Massacre

years the pervasive fear that his father would not return, and that the children were kept close, warned that if they went too far from camp, "The Wasicus (the whites) might get you."[18]

Eyck arrived at the site to find mutilated bodies "freezing into grotesque positions."[19] As he watched the Indians leaving the battlefield, they turned and jeered him, daring him to come down into the flat and fight with them. Eyck knew better than to respond to such goading. When the Indians were gone, heading to Peno Valley, he took back 49 bodies.

To Carrington, logic dictated that the Indian force would return within a day to attack the fort, now weakened by the loss of one third of its forces. Carrington's viewpoint was, for the most part, based on Civil War thinking, which saw regiments hurl themselves against immovable barriers and overwhelming fire, such as in Pickett's Charge at Gettysburg. However, lunging at the heart of an enemy's defense with massive force was not the Indian way, and not typical of any form of guerilla warfare.

Nevertheless, when Carrington received news of Fetterman's fate, he prepared for an all-out assault, and sent word to Fort Laramie with a lone rider, John "Portugee" Phillips, who volunteered for the mission. Laramie lay 240 miles away, and Phillips would have to endure torturous winter conditions. In an astonishing feat of endurance, Phillips arrived in Laramie only four days later. He wore multiple layers of clothing and was wrapped in a buffalo hide coat. He entered Fort Laramie at 11:00 pm on Christmas night, interrupting a full-dress garrison ball.

At Fort Phil Kearny, Carrington himself led the detail to recover the remainder of the soldiers' bodies, and a blizzard set in as he returned to the fort, postponing the inevitable attack. However, he continued preparations for such an assault by storing extra ammunition and powder in the magazine. Women and children were instructed to go there if the Indians broke through the walls, at which time the magazine would be detonated. Assuming the worst if white women or children were captured, taking their own lives was the only reasonable alternative.

Word spread quickly through military channels, and through the press. General Cooke received the news in Omaha, Nebraska, and with no knowledge of the facts, he blamed Carrington without hesitation. Seizing the initiative in the U.S. Army was commendable if successful, but those who failed were generally either labeled as disobedient, neglectful, or cowardly. Carrington, harboring many valid grievances against the higher ranks, could not point an accusing finger at his superiors. Most of his reports were mysteriously delayed or misplaced, so to place the blame on Fetterman's unruly character was the only alternative available. In support of such a charge, Carrington added the reminder that fellow officer Captain Brown was "eager for Red Cloud's scalp."[20] At one point, Carrington considered charging Captain Powell with complicity in the disappearance of his reports. In pursuit of that charge, he met with Ulysses S. Grant himself, who wouldn't hear of such a serious offense levied against a fellow officer. Carrington subsequently shifted his suspicion to Grant as the leading conspirator in the Army's effort to vilify him.

In the wake of the massacre, Cooke replaced Carrington with Lieutenant Colonel Henry W. Wessells, who headed the relief column to Fort Phil Kearny, ironically bringing supplies and the long-needed extra ammunition. Grant replaced Cooke less than a year later.

With Cooke added to Carrington's list of suspects who either suppressed his accounts of the massacre or held him negligent for not sending any, Carrington's case took on the appearance of a widespread military conspiracy. In hindsight, he may not have been entirely incorrect in such

---

[18] Monnett, Eyewitness to the Fetterman Fight

[19] Exploring Off the Beaten Path

[20] Calitri, Free Republic

an assumption. Captain William H. Bisbee, aide to General Cooke in Omaha, made certain at virtually every opportunity that all information leaving department headquarters incriminated Carrington as the lone guilty party, rather than Fetterman. Cooke's staff further implied that Carrington was a habitual coward. An alliance between Captain Powell and Bisbee became apparent as part of a concerted effort to scapegoat Carrington for the catastrophe. Carrington was reassigned to Fort Casper, and he had the misfortune of leading his forces and their families out of Fort Phil Kearny in another blizzard. Several in his party lost fingers and toes from frostbite along the way.

As the *New York Tribune* and other papers sensationalized the massacre half a continent away, no one in the journalistic world seemed able to get the facts straight, any more than the Army could. Another publication claimed that the battle took place at the very gates of the fort, with the victims screaming to get in while those behind the walls watched. In Margaret Carrington's writings, later used by the investigation panel, a series of "eyewitness articles" were cited, written by individuals who could not have possibly been near the fort or known anyone who was. The only absolutions offered were handed down by Commissioner Louis V. Bogy, who put out a statement that "friendly Indians"[21] should remain disassociated from the event and treated gently, and that even the attackers were "rendered desperate by starvation."[22] President Andrew Johnson ordered an immediate investigation, which resulted in the eventual withdrawal of American forces from the Powder River region, and from the Bozeman Trail.

The investigation, urged on by the embarrassment suffered by the military branches of the United States, asked a host of unanswerable questions and arrived at a body of conclusions that were often not entirely supportable. In the initial phase of the proceedings, Fetterman was cast as the victim, but many suggested that Carrington, seeing his career suddenly endangered, turned to paint Fetterman as an "arrogant fire-eater."[23] Pro-Carrington figures characterized Fetterman as being contemptuous of authority and scornful of the fighting capabilities of the Plains Indian, despite or because of his inexperience. The subject of Fetterman's boast loomed large as each witness expressed his or her memory of it, and the sentiment began to shift, painting Fetterman as reckless. Margaret Carrington's journal claimed that Fetterman declared shortly after his arrival, "A company of regulars could whip a thousand, and a regiment could whip the whole army of hostile tribes."[24] She added that both Captain Brown and Lieutenant Grummond strongly seconded the boast, and that the officer corps was filled with "much parlor bluster,"[25] what she termed as "patriotic pedantry."[26] At the same time, by reminding the readers that the American Army officer viewed himself as an elite of society, and that grandiosity among the ranks was "a common personality trait,"[27] Margaret Carrington unwittingly supported Fetterman's personal nature as being nothing out of the ordinary. Colonel Carrington's only memory of Fetterman's boast was that he declared, "I can take 80 men and go to Tongue River."[28]

However common grandiose "parlor bluster" may have been in such situations, the comment was not lost in the general conversation. Even Jim Bridger heard of it while he was far from the region, through an aged scout named Phillip Faribault Wells, and he in turn passed it on in

[21] 3rd 1000, The Fetterman Massacre
[22] 3rd 1000, The Fetterman Massacre
[23] Exploring Off the Beaten Path
[24] Exploring Off the Beaten Path
[25] Exploring Off the Beaten Path
[26] Exploring Off the Beaten Path
[27] Exploring Off the Beaten Path
[28] Exploring Off the Beaten Path

various remarks. Upon the death of Margaret Carrington, Colonel Carrington married the widow of Lieutenant George Grummond, killed in the ambush. Frances Grummond, now Frances Carrington, repeated the boast in a book published decades later entitled, *My Army Life: A Soldier's Wife at Fort Phil Kearny*. She wrote that Fetterman was emphatic on demonstrating to the Army that the new garrison was entirely unafraid to "meet the Indians or anyone else."[29]

In the Sanborn Commission investigation of 1867, the year following the massacre, Colonel Carrington's testimony was regarded as inconclusive. His characterization of Fetterman as "hot-headed[30] and a "reckless subordinate"[31] was successful at first. Carrington and a sufficient number of officers continued to maintain that Fetterman disobeyed a direct order, and that the case was a simple one on that basis.

Through ongoing research in the following century, history proved unkind to both Carrington and Fetterman. Clearly, the highest-ranking officer's grasp on his command was a loose one. He was seen by his men as a "paper pusher."[32] Separate from the question of whether the order to pursue was given or not, the overarching instructions from headquarters were to conduct an aggressive winter campaign against the tribes, in their camps. A new theory infers that Carrington, in a sudden burst of courage, ordered Fetterman to engage and pursue the raiding party, but was stricken with second thoughts in the following seconds. That would explain, according to some, why he sent Grummond with the "reminder."

Research undertaken in the 21st century tends toward a somewhat more sympathetic view of Fetterman's position among some, but it widens the debate for others. The common view of the massacre has for many years held that Fetterman was not only a fool but a maniac, the way in which Carrington regularly described him. With the infamous boast figuring so prominently in the inquiry, Fetterman was often blithely tagged as "a victim of his own dysfunctional degree of boastful chauvinism." However, in his citations for gallant conduct in previous actions, nothing in his service record spoke of carelessness or recklessness. Moreover, as Fetterman himself had noted, he was soon to join with the 27th Cavalry, and finally rid himself of what he saw as an ineffectual commander in Henry Carrington. One might wonder why he had any reason for risking a stain on his record for direct disobedience of orders when he was likely to be free of Carrington in short order anyway. The inquiry grappled with the question of Fetterman's choice of such a location for glory, a "small and fleeting gratification"[33] in defying a commanding officer for whom he had no respect. Fetterman certainly realized that disobeying a direct order and seizing the initiative were entirely separate matters. Finally, despite his combat inexperience on the frontier, he was well acquainted with Indian decoy tactics, and he had always exercised caution around such raids. To some military experts, the only fault in Fetterman's maneuvers during the attack was in assuming that enemy numbers would be what they had always been in the past. Furthermore, Carrington's public view that Fetterman had acted "ignorantly and defiantly"[34] was rendered questionable by the determination that once Fetterman headed over the ridge, Carrington had more than sufficient time in which to bring him back. According to those who watched Fetterman's unit disappear from view, Carrington showed no reaction to suggest that his orders were being ignored.

---

[29] History.com

[30] Monnett, History.Net

[31] Exploring Off the Beaten Path

[32] Exploring Off the Beaten Path

[33] History.Net.com

[34] Exploring Off the Beaten Path

The investigation into the massacre took its toll on other survivors as well. Some accused Captain Ten Eyck of tarrying to the extreme on his way to rescue Fetterman, Brown, and Grummond. Eyck purportedly took a longer route to the top of the ridge, and proceeded at a methodical speed. Some in the military deemed such an approach to fit well into the category of "justifiable military prudence."[35] Others accused him of cowardice and drunkenness, but in the end, he was able to retire quietly from the Army. In hindsight, most reenactments of the massacre as it was thought to unfold suggest that Eyck would never have arrived in time to save Fetterman, nor would his company have fared any better against the enemy numbers present.

Lieutenant Grummond fared poorly throughout the ensuing investigations as well, although the logic of a late arrival is supported by the condition of mounts at Fort Phil Kearny. Grummond was allegedly leading a unit of raw recruits. For many, Powell's relief action for the woodcutters two days before was the first action the new men had seen, and despite all available horses being kept at the ready, the supply had been raided for several months prior on a regular basis. By December, deliveries of feed grain became sporadic, and extra horses were needed for escort and mail duty. To have immediate use of the necessary number of mounts was likely impractical by December 21. According to several accounts, Carrington sent Grummond out to "tell"[36] Fetterman to stay on the fort side of the ridge, rather than to merely remind him. It is further alleged that Carrington spoke with Grummond again shortly before his departure, saying, "Don't leave him."[37]

On top of that, the commission questioned the efficacy of giving Grummond such an important rank, especially considering his suspicious background. Before the Plains actions, he was promoted on multiple occasions for acts of recklessness that turned out well, despite his poor judgment. Along the way, he was frequently cited for "violent and drunken behavior off-duty,"[38] for which he was once court-martialed and subsequently reprimanded. The charges against him included a propensity for abusive acts against civilians.

Grummond's personal life did not suit the profile for a U.S. Army officer. While his wife Delia was pregnant at home in Tennessee with their second child, he was soon courting a "beautiful Union sympathizer"[39] named Frances, who eventually became his second wife. As his dalliance in the West continued, Delia filed for divorce and a settlement of $2,000 for failing to support his family.

Grummond's dangerous professional behavior revealed itself again at Fort Phil Kearny. In the December 6 raid, he blatantly disobeyed a direct order, leaving his detachment to pursue a lone Indian riding an injured horse. This action led four soldiers under his command to lose their lives, and likely inspired the Sioux to continue employing the tactic of decoys. Ultimately, even though he was relieved of command for a time, he was brought back by Carrington due to an absence of available officers. More than one source noted that Grummond appeared "unconcerned"[40] with either the legal suits against him, or with professional repercussions on any front. By the time he had been married to Frances for 20 days, a judgment reached him from Detroit ruling in favor of his first wife. He proceeded to flee his financial obligations and applied for a position with the Foreign Service, then accepted a commission as Second Lieutenant,

[35] WikiVisually

[36] Calitri, Free Republic

[37] Calitri, Free Republic

[38] Calitri, Free Republic

[39] Calitri, Free Republic

[40] Calitri, Free Republic

bringing him to Fort Phil Kearny.

The U.S. Army investigated the Fetterman Massacre at length, in part from a need to set the historical and military record straight, and to assess proper blame. General Sherman was particularly shocked that Carrington cited a lack of support in men and materials from headquarters. To blame higher-ups was poor form. However, of more long-term importance was the question of the Bozeman Trail's efficacy as an institution to be maintained, how it was lost in the first place, and whether anything could or should be done about it.

The End of Red Cloud's War

When the Bozeman Trail was closed in the wake of the Fetterman Massacre, one experienced traveler remarked, "Last year the Reno and Phil Kearny route was pronounced open for emigration, and hundreds of graves along its entire length with the Phil Kearny massacre as the central figure, attest how the promise was kept with the emigrants. This year it is accepted as hostile and impossible."[xcvi]

Another consequence of the massacre was that it forced the Crow's hand. As a result of the humiliating defeat at the hands of the Sioux, many Crow leaders feared the Army would abandon the forts along the Bozeman Trail, leaving them to the mercy of Red Cloud's allies.[xcvii] At the same time, the Army's defeat did not bolster the Crow's confidence in the government's ability to even protect them in the first place.[xcviii]

The Sioux, in turn, warned the Crow to flee the areas around the forts lest they become fully embroiled in the war. This placed the Crow in a serious quandary. On the one hand, their token support of the Army by serving as messengers and scouts placed them under Sioux fire.[xcix] On the other hand, the Crow despised the Sioux, and though they refused to serve as messengers after the Fetterman Massacre, those who had aligned with the Sioux broke off relations with their old enemies. This strange middle ground was partially solved when Captain Kinney directly hired 10 Crow scouts and spies, separating their actions from those of their tribe.[c]

Despite repeated warnings, the Crow remained around Fort C. F. Smith, and the Sioux in turn left them alone. Captain Kinney noted at the time that the Crow's presence at the fort may very well have saved it from a fate similar to Fetterman's, for as revealed earlier, there were plenty of hostile natives along the Trail to cause trouble if they desired it.[ci] Still, the winter of 1866-67 was relatively peaceful, likely thanks to the harsh Plains' winter as much as anything else.

As the season warmed, the American Army's Crow scouts proved how safe they felt in the region, ignoring their courier duties to scout and report buffalo herd movements, something far more important to them than the war. With the coming of the buffalo, so too came the natives, and hostilities quickly picked up as the weather warmed.[cii]

Throughout the winter, the U.S. government attempted to initiate peace with Red Cloud's federation, but he rebuffed them each time. To the Sioux leader, there would be peace when the whites left the Powder River Country and abandoned the Bozeman Trail and the hated forts, not before.[ciii] Thus the war continued, with the Crow maintaining their precarious neutrality while the Army fought and died to maintain the Bozeman Trail.

Though the Sioux and their allies never attacked Fort C. F. Smith proper, the surrounding areas were fair game, and on August 1, 1867, a force of roughly 500 Cheyenne attacked a group of 30 civilian hay cutters outside the fort. Cut off and surrounded, the civilians managed to keep the natives at bay, inflicting light casualties before the natives retreated.[civ] The next day, the natives attacked the area surrounding the resupplied Fort Phil Kearny, surrounding a group of wood-cutters but ultimately retreating once more.[cv] Though it could be argued the natives lost both these battles tactically, the Bozeman Trail remained officially closed which for the natives was of course the point.[cvi]

Native accounts of Red Cloud's War are relatively sparse, but there are several accounts from American sources, and one source went into detail on what's now known as the Wagon Box Fight. As a participant in that engagement, a soldier who was part of the escort from the fort explained how the local contractors formed a corral to protect their livestock about six miles west of the fort, using the boxes from their wagons to form a primitive enclosure to herd the animals at night.[cvii] The corral, situated close by the woods and the tents, held a large supply of ammunition, so that in the event of attack the workers could rally to the corral for defense.[cviii]

On August 1, following the Hayfield Fight, a sergeant questioned the woodcutters' escort to see if they had seen any Indians. The soldiers replied they had not.[cix] Though the night pickets saw nothing, one of their dogs repeatedly ran down the hill "barking and snapping furiously."[cx] The dog's instincts and picket's hindsight proved the natives lurked in the darkness, waiting for the perfect moment to strike.

Shortly after the participant started his morning picket duty, around 7:00 am, that moment arrived.[cxi] Alerted to the presence of the attack by a shout, the soldiers readied themselves for battle as seven mounted natives approached from the north in single file, chanting a war song along the way.[cxii] Having just been issued new rifles, and having yet to fire them in anger, the soldiers took care to adjust their sights and ready their weapons for battle, a fault with Army training and supplies throughout the Indian Wars. After taking their shots, the pickets looked toward the camp and saw "to the foothills toward the north... more Indians than we had ever seen before."[cxiii]

With no orders to move, the pickets decided to retreat to the corral, utilizing a simple staggered volley fire as they headed for safety. It did not take long for the natives to bring their own weapons to bear, and the soldier who left the account barely got the drop on a native with a Spencer carbine, who fired a shot that just missed him while the soldier downed the native.[cxiv] Still the pickets ran, joining with one of the contractors in their retreat while the natives "increased in numbers at such an alarming rate that they seemed to rise out of the ground like a flock of birds."[cxv]

Though the natives rushed to cut the pickets off from the corral, the small group got within firing distance, and thanks to one of the sergeants sallying out to provide covering fire, managed to reach the corral's limited safety.[cxvi] Finding the escort company's commander, our participant, wheezing for breath, explained why he abandoned his picket station without orders –a crime normally punished by firing squad. The captain lauded the man for his efforts, declaring, "You'll have to fight for your lives today!"[cxvii] Thus rallied, the soldiers and civilians prepared to fend off an unknown horde of natives, their only defense Government Issue wood boxes in the same style and construction that was used in the Civil War.[cxviii]

The natives came, and the soldiers opened fire as the Indians circled and galloped around them, firing bullets and arrows at the defenders. Despite increasing casualties, the natives' attack continued, and the defenders kept up their fire until finally the natives gathered their dead and withdrew.[cxix] They returned not long after, however, utilizing the cover of the tents near the corral to block their assault. Risking enemy fire, our participant and several others sallied from the corral to down the tents and open the soldier's field of vision, and thus their field of fire.[cxx]

The battle continued into the afternoon, with water and ammunition running scarce and fire arrows threatening the corral. A massive assault of natives on foot threatened to end the fight in their favor, but the soldiers' fire slowly ground them down.[cxxi] On the brink of being overwhelmed, the natives, unused to Western style fighting and preferring less costly skirmish combat, broke and fled. Our participant noted that throughout the battle, Red Cloud himself observed "on top of a ridge due east of our little improvised fort."[cxxii] A large portion of the remaining soldiers opened fire on the observing war leader but missed, hitting the warriors scattered below him instead. Finally, with the rallying blast of a howitzer from Fort Phil Kearny heralding reinforcements, the natives withdrew for good, having sustained heavy casualties while inflicting far fewer in number than received. [cxxiii]

G. Coudert's picture of the scene of the Wagon Box Fight

A monument at the scene of the skirmish

Despite these kinds of battles, as well as official warnings and the actual closing of the Trail, some enterprising if foolhardy traders still braved it, some even successfully. A trader by the name of Nelson Story took advantage of the fact that the natives stole horses instead of oxen, the primary beast of burden used to haul wagons across the various trails westward, to supply C. F. Smith throughout Red Cloud's War.[cxxiv] For the duration of the war, Story managed to successfully trade with the fort unmolested, though this was in part because he never traveled east of the fort, where the Sioux ran rampant.[cxxv]

Story

For the Crow, the use of couriers seemed to tip the hand of the Sioux, not only frustrated by the Crow's friendliness to the Army, but also the Army's continued presence in the Powder River Country despite their best efforts.[cxxvi] While war raged on in the Plains, the federal government authorized a commission to meet the natives in July 1867, marking another attempt to end the war. The commission failed; bolstered by the success of the Fetterman Massacre at the war's onset, and further emboldened by a lack of reprisal, Red Cloud's War continued and intensified.[cxxvii]

While peace commissions to Red Cloud failed, other commissions bore better fruit. In the winter of 1867, the Secretary of the Interior formed a committee to investigate the causes of Red Cloud's War, both to see if it was worth the cost in lives and to investigate the validity of rumors of Crow involvement in Fetterman's Massacre. Exacerbating the issue, the settlers of the Gallatin Valley near the Trail, though never assaulted or threatened by Red Cloud's forces, continued to clamor for increased military presence and protection.[cxxviii]

While the committee deliberated, the Honorable Judge John F. Kinney traveled west to meet directly with the Crow.[cxxix] Kinney, stationed at Fort Laramie, had some trouble convincing the Crow to leave the safety of Fort C. F. Smith, but eventually the two sides met at Fort Laramie, though the Crow, suspecting Sioux hostility against them, refused to travel further south.[cxxx] Kinney arrived on May 31, only to discover most of the Crow delegation departed for a buffalo hunt, its timing possibly hastened by a Sioux raid that had succeeded in capturing over 40 Crow ponies.[cxxxi]

Kinney

Kinney's arrival marked a watershed for American relations with the Crow and Sioux. Crow neutrality had upset the Sioux and lowered the confidence of the Army in one of their few native allies. Fort C. F. Smith received a new commander, Lieutenant Colonel Luther Bradley, who looked on the Crow's supposed neutrality with suspicion.[cxxxii] Kinney, meanwhile, heard out the Crow's precarious plight, learning that while the Crow would fight their old enemy the Sioux, Lakota aggression required they reopen negotiations for a more formal truce with their fellow natives, lest they earn Red Cloud's wrath.[cxxxiii]

Sympathetic to the Crow's plight, Kinney recommended the Crow receive extended protection from the U.S. government, as well as rations and reimbursement for horses lost in Sioux raids. Most importantly, he advocated returning the former Crow lands back to them.[cxxxiv] It should be noted this final recommendation did have the now familiar ulterior motive of meaning the Bozeman Trail would be within the lands of a presumably friendly native tribe. Though the Crow hated the Trail as much as any other tribe, Kinney may have hoped that increased American support would temper the Crow's feelings about it. As a further gesture, Kinney dispatched an interpreter and trader to join the Crow camp to help deflect Sioux overtures.[cxxxv]

Based on subsequent Crow actions, it can be surmised they responded positively to Kinney's overtures, bringing them closer to the Army and further from their Sioux enemies. Crow intelligence was critical in the string of victories in early August of 1867, especially the Hayfield Fight and Wagon Box Fight.[cxxxvi]

Despite such victories as the Wagon Box Fight, the war continued, and native skirmishing tactics proved their worth when it came to forcing the Army to abandon the forts and leave the Bozeman Trail to its original owners. Unfortunately for the Crow, Sioux aggression grew too powerful to ignore. Kinney's delegation and a handful of loyal Crow remained while the bulk of the tribe quietly slipped away from Fort C. F. Smith.[cxxxvii]

Despite Kinney's best efforts to sway the Crow fully to the American side, the tribe maintained neutrality in fear of Sioux retribution. The conclusion of Kinney's Crow delegation was that unless the U.S. committed sufficient troops to attack Red Cloud's forces offensively, rather than holing up defensively in an increasingly impotent gesture of defiance, the Crow would abandon the Americans.[cxxxviii]

Fortunately for the Americans, Sioux hostility overcame Army impotence, and the Crow formally sided with them against the Sioux. Unfortunately, the previously mentioned committee seemed willing to acknowledge the Sioux conquest of the Powder River Country, rather than the old land claims outlined in the 1851 Fort Laramie Treaty.[cxxxix] Some even spoke of abandoning the Bozeman Trail altogether, though such talk occurred before the victories in early August. Kinney, seeing the return of the Powder River Country as the first step to civilizing the Crow, continued to advocate in their favor.[cxl]

In July of 1867, again before the victories in August, a commission was formed with the stated goal of negotiating an end to Red Cloud's War. While the commission was organized, it sent word to the tribes to meet at Fort Laramie, something many of the younger Crow vehemently opposed.[cxli] With summer slowly giving way to autumn, the Crow also grew restless to begin preparation hunting for winter, something the rampant Sioux could easily hinder. Still, the Crow continued to support the Army, delivering mail between forts for a hefty sum of $33.33 per month.[cxlii]

All the while, with Sioux running rampant across the country, the Crow faced the real possibility of starvation from the inability to hunt in safety. To bolster their native allies, the U.S. supplied the Crow with cattle and flour to support them through the winter as the autumn of 1867 became the winter of 1868.[cxliii]

The commission's efforts to gather the tribal leaders bore fruit in November of 1867, thanks largely to the Sioux's willingness to suspend hostilities so the Crow could make the 327 mile trek to Fort Laramie.[cxliv] As a prelude to further negotiations to end the war, the commission started negotiating revised formal dealings with the Crow. The U.S. opened negotiations by suggesting the Crow sell their lands in exchange for farming, building supplies and teachers "so that your children may become as intelligent as the whites."[cxlv] The delicate matters of the Bozeman Trail and Sioux control of former Crow lands never came up at this early juncture, though the negotiators offered to allow the Crow to hunt on the lands so long as there were buffalo to hunt.[cxlvi]

The Crow response was a vehement reminder of the damage done to the land and game by the Americans; of animals hunted to deprive them to the natives, or forests cleared for settlers and forts, and lands scorched for farming. Concluding his impassioned speech, the Crow leader Bear's Tooth rhetorically asked, "[I]f I went into your country to kill your animals, what would you say?"[cxlvii] Rejecting the notion of "civilizing" that the whites offered, the Crow leaders made clear their suspicions when it came to signing any more treaties with the Americans. They also made clear their dislike of the Bozeman Trail, stating to the commission they should "recall your young men who have camped all along this path and all those who seek for gold. They are the cause of all our wars and misfortunes."[cxlviii] Reiterated passionately over three hours, the first meeting of the commission with the Crow did not go as well as the commission hoped.[cxlix]

The two sides continued back and forth, with the commission adamant that the Crow select a reservation while they still had a choice in the matter, but the Crow remained equally as adamant that they would maintain their traditional lifestyle as long as the buffalo roamed the Plains.[cl] Offered a treaty, the Crow refused to sign on three grounds: the lack of Sioux present at the negotiating table; the treaty's failure to mention closing the Bozeman Trail; and the fact that not all Crow leaders were present to discuss the treaty.[cli] Reaching a stalemate, the commission took minor solace in managing to obtain an agreement to reconvene at Fort Phil Kearny in the spring of 1868.[clii]

Before Red Cloud's War, the Crow desired the removal of the Sioux from the Powder River Country, but now, the Crow merely desired the closure of the Bozeman Trail as condition for their continued support and friendship. This change in view reflected the increasing tension between the Americans and the natives. As the Americans put pressure on the natives to civilize, the Crow pushed back with a desire to keep to their old ways.[cliii] The Bozeman Trail represented everything the Crow grew to dislike in their American allies, most notably the scattered game, a land gouged by wagon wheels, and an increased military presence. Such was the state of relations that closing the Trail became more important to the Crow than reclaiming the Powder River Country.[cliv] In this regard, the Crow had more in common with Red Cloud's alliance than with the American government.

Despite the common grounds, the Crow remained firm in their opposition to the Sioux, and as 1867 turned to 1868, the American government once more prepared for peace. Lacking the manpower to defend the Trail in its entirety, and unwilling to forsake what little goodwill remained with one of their few native allies, preparations began for another peace conference to end Red Cloud's War. This time the Americans were willing to close the Bozeman Trail and permanently abandon the three forts in Powder River Country.[clv]

Reaching Fort Laramie on April 10, the peace conference contained the American delegation, Crow leaders, and representatives from the Cheyenne and Arapaho. Noticeably absent were Red Cloud and his Sioux allies, who refused to appear until well after the three forts were abandoned.[clvi]

One by one, the three forts emptied. Fort Reno succumbed to a mysterious fire not long after its evacuation, with little remaining but a few walls and scorched earth.[clvii] Fort C. F. Smith, once a bastion of U.S.-Crow relations, also emptied. Finally, Fort Phil Kearny, the "hated post on the Little Piney," where the war began and some of its greatest battles were fought, was also evacuated, also succumbing to a fire shortly afterward.[clviii] With the progress of the Union Pacific Railroad westward, the Bozeman Trail became obsolete, and so the Trail lay to return to its native owners, a wagon trail once more a game trail.

The 1868 Treaty of Fort Laramie set the boundaries of the reservations in and around the Powder River Country, and it further stated that "the United States now solemnly agrees that no persons except those herein designated and authorized so to do, and except such officers, agents, and employees of the Government as may be authorized to enter upon Indian reservations in discharge of duties enjoined by law, shall ever be permitted to pass over, settle upon, or reside in the territory described in this article…"[clix] The Treaty also included standard declarations for support infrastructure and tradesmen, requirements of educating children, relinquishing lands beyond the reservation, and eventual transition of the natives into landowners, as such treaties often did.[clx]

The Crow, incidentally, found themselves more or less hung out to dry, for the Treaty expressly granted the Powder River Country to the Sioux, abandoning the long-time goal of reclaiming the Crow's old homelands.[clxi] The new Treaty reduced Crow lands from the 38 million acres of the 1851 Treaty to 8 million acres. In exchange, the American government agreed to provide an agency, doctors, teachers, four years of provisions, and aid in transferring from a nomadic lifestyle to agriculture.[clxii]

The 1868 Treaty left a bitter taste in many mouths. The soldiers from the forts felt betrayed by the government that abandoned the forts they'd fought and bled to defend.[clxiii] The Crow felt betrayed for their lost lands, though they also took solace in the closure of the Bozeman Trail, a sore point in relations since the Trail's forging.[clxiv]

By November of 1867, Red Cloud recognized that he could not sustain his offensive against so many of the enemy carrying such improved weaponry. However, he also understood the waning spirit for U.S. military commitment to the Bozeman Trail, and the larger Powder River region. Following the Fetterman Massacre and Wagon Box Fight, the U.S. government entered into a treaty with Lakota and Arapaho leaders at Fort Laramie in 1868. Red Cloud was the last of the Native American leaders to sign this treaty, which allegedly guaranteed that the Lakota Sioux would own the Black Hills (Paha Sapa) of South Dakota in perpetuity, and that area would be set aside for Native Americans only. Whites could not enter the territory without the express permission of the Sioux, which was essential because the Black Hills are the "holy land" of Lakota and other indigenous peoples. In addition, the treaty dictated that the U.S. Army would abandon forts along the Bozeman Trail. In exchange for American abandonment of the Bozeman Trail, the tribes agreed to allow the building and use of railroads. They promised to cease all attacks against American citizens, to stop the practice of abducting women and children, and to avoid the killing or scalping of all white men.

Following the years of protracted siege against Fort Kearny, Red Cloud returned to a quieter life. He was the first and last of the Native American chiefs to win a war against the United States. Though the victory would not last, the immediate results spoke for themselves, as the forts were gone and the Trail was closed.

With the Union Pacific Railroad's construction protected by the Treaty, the need for the Bozeman Trail ceased. The coming of the railroads rendered the various trails more or less obsolete across the Plains. The Bozeman Trail, soaked in the blood of natives protesting it, soldiers defending it, and even its namesake, now lay to return to the land and the natives who claimed it, unmolested by pioneers, soldiers, or prospectors.

The Aftermath

In 1870, Red Cloud traveled to New York City and Washington D.C., speaking to crowds and explaining both his people's plight and his understanding of the Treaty of Fort Laramie of 1868. It was during this trip that Red Cloud became convinced his people could never overcome the American settlers, based on their numbers and their great cities. However, his speeches in the East were sufficient to raise public awareness and led to the alteration of the original treaty. In fact, he became something of an exotic celebrity during this time, and he held peace negotiations with high-level American representatives over the following two decades. Many of his people were offended by this striking turnaround, during which their chief met with the American president. He was accused by some of "selling out,"[41] while government officials with whom he met secretly later believed he directed and helped the Sioux and Cheyenne defeat Custer at the Battle of the Little Bighorn a decade after the Fetterman Massacre.

General George Cooke returned to the Bozeman Trail in three campaigns against the same tribes with which the Army had signed a new treaty. After an astonishing number of dead in the region between the Sioux, Cheyenne, Arapaho, and the Army, the Bozeman Trail was rendered all but useless. The Transcontinental Railroad was completed, and transportation westward changed forever.

In 1870, Henry Carrington left the army for civilian life. Never suited to the path of a career soldier, he took a position on the faculty of Wabash College in military science. Margaret Carrington died that year, probably of tuberculosis. With Frances as his second wife since 1871, Carrington officially adopted the son of Lieutenant Grummond, and the couple went on to raise three more children. Frances was 20 years Carrington's junior.

---

[41] Northwest Plains Reservation and Biographies of Plains Indians – www.nativepartnership.org/site/PageServer?pagename=airc_bio_main

Even by the time Carrington left the service, the 1868 treaty was being broken, and when an expedition into the Black Hills led by Lieutenant Colonel George Custer discovered gold in 1874, miners flooded into the region in violation of the treaty. The Lakota, hunting within the confines of the territory promised to them by the treaty, began encountering white settlers and attacked them. Red Cloud considered it his right and that of his people to defend the territory that had been conceded to them in perpetuity by the treaty, and the Sioux warriors' ambushes created a virtual no-man's land within the Black Hills. White horse thieves and bandits also occupied the region, preying upon other trespassers and Native Americans alike. In response, whites demanded protection by the U.S. Army, which had been complying with the treaty and ejected the white interlopers.

Custer

The removal of white miners had the effect of increasing political pressure on the government to open the Black Hills to mining, logging, and settlement. In May of 1875, Red Cloud joined several other Lakota leaders traveled to Washington in the hope of convincing President Grant to honor the treaty conditions. In response, the government attempted to purchase the Black Hills for $25,000.

Later that year, Grant met with Major General Philip Sheridan and Brigadier General George Crook, and the three agreed to end the policy of ejecting miners and settlers. Also, the president and the generals decided to notify Native American groups not already residing on the reservations that they had until January 31, 1876, to surrender to authorities and settle on reservations. The concept of ultimatums was foreign to Native Americans, and many bands were so far from existing reservations that they would be hard pressed to make it onto reservations before the deadline had passed. Red Cloud led one of these free bands that refused to report to the reservation.

After the January 31, 1876 deadline came and went, the U.S. Army sent two columns of troops under General Crook and General Alfred Terry, and a third column commanded by Colonel John Gibbon, into the region in March of 1876. The force was composed of 10 companies of cavalry and two companies of infantry, dispatched to provide protection for civilians mining in the Back Hills. However, the U.S. troops were caught in a blizzard, and the majority of them were forced to abandon their pack train. Also, the force suffered a number of frostbite casualties. General Terry's column stalled, but part of Crook's command, Colonel Joseph J. Reynolds with six companies of cavalry, located a Native American village consisting of about 65 lodges and attacked it in mid-March. The Reynolds force believed they had located and attacked the band led by Crazy Horse, but in fact they had attacked a Cheyenne village. Prior to the attack, the village's occupants had been allied with the United States against the Lakota and other Native American bands. In fact, the Cheyenne, whose homes had been destroyed, had been rushing to the reservation in compliance with the government order. After the attack, the Cheyenne became fierce enemies of the white settlers, and Lakota followers of Sitting Bull offered some of the Cheyenne refuge. The attack again demonstrated the inability of U.S. troops to distinguish between friend and foe among Native Americans.

George Crook

Sitting Bull

This set in motion the chain of events that would lead to the fateful Battle of the Rosebud Creek and the Battle of the Little Bighorn, the latter being the most famous battle of the Indian Wars. One of the biggest military debacles in American history, the battle is notorious and controversial for the annihilation of the U.S. 7th Cavalry at the hands of warriors led by Sitting Bull, Crazy Horse, and Chief Galt. How Custer met his fate, and whether there was even a Last Stand, remain subjects of debate, but what is known is that the Battle of the Little Bighorn was one of the U.S. military's worst defeats. All told, the 7th Cavalry suffered over 50% casualties, with over 250 men killed and over 50 wounded. In the aftermath of the 7th Cavalry's decimation and the complete destruction of Custer's force, the American public was incensed. The people's ire was probably inflamed by the fact that news reached the East just as the nation was celebrating its centennial.

By 1878 the Oglala band had been moved to the Pine Ridge Agency, where Red Cloud would live for the rest of his life. Dr. James Irwin resigned as Indian Agent effective January 1, 1879, and he would be replaced later that spring by Valentine McGillycuddy. The agency was deliberately renamed to minimize Red Cloud's association with it in the hopes of reducing his influence.

On December 28, 1890, Big Foot's band of Lakota surrendered to U.S. troops at the Pine Ridge Reservation. They were escorted to the Wounded Knee Creek, where the 350 Native Americans established a camp. Big Foot's band was composed mostly of the widows, relatives, and children of warriors killed during the great Sioux War of 1876-1877. On the morning of December 29, 1890, soldiers approached the Big Foot encampment, with orders to disarm the Lakota and burn the weapons. Allegedly, when a soldier attempted to disarm a warrior who happened to be deaf, the Native Americans lack of response triggered an attack. It remains unclear which side fired the first shot. It was clear after the commencement of shooting and killing some 290 of the mostly unarmed Lakota men, women, and children were not protected by the "Ghost Shirts" many wore. The Ghost Dance movement held that sacred "Ghost Shirts" were bulletproof and would render the wearer invincible, and at least one holy man at the Wounded Knee camp was advocating armed resistance based on this idea. In the aftermath of the Wounded Knee Massacre, it was clear that the "Ghost Shirts" offered no protection whatsoever from the soldiers' firearms.

After initially supporting the Ghost Dance movement, Red Cloud began to urge his people to abandon the practice in the wake of the Wounded Knee Massacre, but as more and more of his Oglala people began to advocate for a return to violence in opposition to white settlement, Red Cloud began to lose influence among his band members. Among those who opposed him were those who recalled his opposition to the Dawes Act of 1877, asserting that he wished to impede his people's progress down the white man's road. Though his influence diminished among his own people, he continued to advocate for the protection of tribal land and push for Native American control over their territory. The traditionalist wanted to maintain power in the hands of the chiefs, and fundamentally disagreed with the United States, regarding who was best fit to direct the progress of indigenous people. He sought to protect his people from the negative aspects of American culture and sought to preserve as much of the "old ways" as possible.

As for the Bozeman Trail, though it merely lasted five years and was closed for two of them, its mark on history and the land had an impact as deep as the wagon gouges dug into its ground. The Bozeman Trail cost soldiers' lives in the aftermath of the deadliest war in American history, fractured good feelings with one of the few native tribes aligned with the government, and exacerbated the hatred and anger felt by other native tribes. The Bozeman Trail's legacy was mostly one of death and betrayal.

That said, it is also a tale of the pioneer spirit, for the Bozeman Trail, like other similar trails, rose from a need to travel west and fill the land so that America could truly stretch from sea to shining sea. Before the country could be filled, those who lived there first had to be shoved out of the way, and the fact that the Bozeman Trail witnessed one of the few times those who were there first managed to push back, even if briefly, makes it all the more important.

Today, the Bozeman Trail is commemorated with historic markers, and modern highways roughly follow its historic path. Interstate 25 in Wyoming, Interstate 90 from Wyoming to Montana (a scant 30 miles from the city that bears the Trail's name), and U.S. Route 287 roughly form a modern Bozeman Trail. They all appear as modern indications that despite the setbacks the Americans suffered there against the Sioux, the Trail, like the West overall, eventually was won.

Online Resources

Other books about Native American history by Charles River Editors

Other books about Red Cloud's War on Amazon

Bibliography

Moulton, Candy: Susan Badger Doyle's two-volume work on the Bozeman Trail blazes some new ground. (Interview with S.B. Doyle). Wild West, Vol. 14, No. 2 (Aug. 2001), p. 56, column II.

Doyle, Susan Badger (Ed.): Journeys to the Land of Gold. Emigrant Diaries from the Bozeman Trail, 1863-1866. Helena, 2000, Vol. 2, p. 743.

Kappler, Charles J.: Indian Affairs. Laws and Treaties. Washington, 1904. Vol. 2, p. 594. http://digital.library.okstate.edu/kappler/Vol2/treaties/sio0594.htm. Utley, Robert M.: The Bozeman Trail before John Bozeman: A busy Land. Montana, The Magazine of Western History, Vol. 53, No. 2 (Summer 2003), pp. 20-31.

Utley, Robert M.: The Bozeman Trail before John Bozeman: A busy Land. Montana, The Magazine of Western History, Vol. 53, No. 2 (Summer 2003), pp. 20-31, quote p. 20.

Kappler, Charles J.: Indian Affairs. Laws and Treaties. Washington, 1904. Vol. 2, p. 594. http://digital.library.okstate.edu/kappler/Vol2/treaties/sio0594.htm.

Rzeczkowski, Frank: The Crow Indians and the Bozeman Trail. Montana, The Magazine of Western History. Vol. 49, No. 4 (Winter 1999), pp. 30-47, quote p.47.

Medicine Crow, Joseph: From the Heart of the Crow Country. New York, 1992, p. 84. Serial 1308, 40th Congress, 1st Session, Vol. 1, Senate Executive Document No. 13, p. 127.

Moulton, Candy: Susan Badger Doyle's two-volume work on the Bozeman Trail blazes some new ground. (Interview with S.B. Doyle). Wild West, Vol. 14, No. 2 (Aug. 2001), p. 56, column I.

Doyle, Susan Badger (Ed.): Journeys to the Land of Gold. Emigrant Diaries from the Bozeman Trail, 1863-1866. Helena, 2000, Vol. 1, p. 1 (total number of travelers); Vol. 1, p. 154 (casualties): Vol. 1, p. XII (altering of route); Vol. 2, p. 744 (guidebook); Vol. 2, p. 759 (mountain fever); Vol. 1, p. 293 (Richard Owen); Vol. 2, p. 767 (organization); Vol. 1, p. 224 (description of train); Vol. 2, p. 435 (ration of women and children); Vol. 1, p. 62 (rate) and Vol 2. p. 435 (freight trains).

"In remembrance of the Bear River Massacre". lemhi-shoshone.com/. Retrieved 2013-11-30.

"Connor Battlefield". Wyoming State Historical Society. Retrieved 2013-11-30.

Doyle, Susan Badger (Ed.): Journeys to the Land of Gold. Emigrant Diaries from the Bozeman Trail, 1863-1866. Helena, 2000, Vol. 2, p. 423.

Kappler, Charles J.: Indian Affairs. Laws and Treaties. Washington, 1904. Vol. 2, p. 594. http://digital.library.okstate.edu/kappler/Vol2/treaties/sio0594.htm

Kennedy, Michael S. (1964). "Tall in the Saddle-First Trail Drive to Montana Territory". Cowboys and Cattlemen-A Roundup from Montana The Magazine of Western History. New York: Hastings House Publishing. pp. 103–111.

Hoxie, Frederick E.: Parading Through History. The making of the Crow Nation in America, 1805-1935. Cambridge, 1995, p. 89.

McGinnis, Anthony: Counting Coup and Cutting Horses. Intertribal Warfare on the Northern Plains, 1738-1889. Evergreen, 1990, p. 114.

Utley, Robert M.: The Bozeman Trail before John Bozeman: A busy Land. Montana, The Magazine of Western History, Vol. 53, No. 2 (Summer 2003), pp. 20-31, quote p. 20.

Hebard, Grace Raymond and E.A. Brininstool: The Bozeman Trail. Glendale, 1960, p. 160. Templeton, George M.: Diaries, 1866-1868, (typescript), The Newberry Library, Chicago, pp. 55,59, 72 and 99.

Rzeczkowski, Frank: The Crow Indians and the Bozeman Trail. Montana, The Magazine of Western History. Vol. 49, No. 4 (Winter 1999), pp. 30-47. Dunlay, Thomas W.: Wolves for the Blue Soldiers. Indian Scouts and Auxiliaries with the United States Army, 1860-1890. Lincoln and London, 1982, p. 39.

Kappler, Charles J.: Indian Affairs. Laws and Treaties. Washington, 1904. Vol. 2 pp. 998-1003. "Archived copy". Archived from the original on 2011-11-26. Retrieved 2011-11-26.. Compare the 1851 Crow treaty territory with the 1868 unceded Indian territory of the Lakotas.

Free Books by Charles River Editors

We have brand new titles available for free most days of the week. To see which of our titles are currently free, click on this link.

Discounted Books by Charles River Editors

We have titles at a discount price of just 99 cents everyday. To see which of our titles are currently 99 cents, click on this link.

Endnotes

[i] Frank Rzeczkowski, "The Crow Indians and the Bozeman Trail", Montana: The Magazine of Western History, Montana Historical Society, pg. 1.

[ii] Ibid, 2.

[iii] Ibid, 2.

[iv] Ibid, 3. There was also going around the continent, but without a canal that trip was long, expensive, and dangerous.

[v] Ibid, 3.

[vi] Ibid, 3.

[vii] Ibid, 3.

[viii] Ibid, 3.

[ix] Hebard, Grace Raymond and E.A. Brininstool: *The Bozeman Trail, Volume 1*. Cleveland, The Arthur H. Clark Company, 1922, pg. 26.

[x] Ibid, 26-28.

[xi] Ibid, 44. The Santa Fe Trail was largely commercial in nature, with most of its traffic being merchants heading west to take advantage of markets stretching from Mexico and the Pacific Ocean.

[xii] Ibid, 214.

[xiii] Ibid, 214-215.

[xiv] Ibid, 215.

[xv] Ibid, 215.

[xvi] Ibid, 215.

[xvii] Ibid, 215.

[xviii] Quoted in Ibid, 216.

[xix] Ibid, 216.

[xx] Ibid, 216-217.

[xxi] Ibid, 219.

[xxii] Ibid, 219.

[xxiii] Ibid, 219.

[xxiv] Hebard, Grace R. and E.A. Brininstool: *The Bozeman Trail: Historical Accounts*, Kindle Edition, 2015, pg. 1154.

xxv Ibid, 220. And a partridge in a pear-tree~.

xxvi Ibid, 113.

xxvii Ibid, 113.

xxviii Hebard, Grace Raymond and E.A. Brininstool: *The Bozeman Trail, Volume 2*. Cleveland, The Arthur H. Clark Company, 1922, pg. 113 -14.

xxix Ibid, 114.

xxx Ibid, 121.

xxxi Ibid, 220.

xxxii Kappler, Charles J.: Indian Affairs. Laws and Treaties. Washington, 1904. Vol. 2, pg. 594.

xxxiii Ibid, pg. 594.

xxxiv Frank Rzeczkowski, "The Crow Indians and the Bozeman Trail", pg. 1.

xxxv Hebard, Grace Raymond and E.A. Brininstool: *The Bozeman Trail*, pg. 221.

xxxvi Ibid, 221-223.

xxxvii Ibid, 223-224. For objectivity and to lead into the following section, I have included the passage in its entirety.

xxxviii Ibid, 225. Americans had long overestimated how much authority tribal chiefs had over their tribes, and though a fascinating subject in its own right, such matters are best left to an anthropologist or historian specializing in such material.

xxxix Frank Rzeczkowski, "The Crow Indians and the Bozeman Trail", 2.

xl Ibid, 2.

xli Ibid, 3.

xlii Ibid, 3.

xliii Ibid, 3.

xliv Ibid, 5.

xlv Hebard, Grace Raymond and E.A. Brininstool: *The Bozeman Trail*, 225-226.

xlvi Ibid, 226.

xlvii Hein, Ellis, "Connor's Powder River Expedition of 1865", Wyoming State Historical Society, https://www.wyohistory.org/encyclopedia/connor%E2%80%99s-powder-river-expedition-1865.

xlviii Ibid. Americans are apparently very bad at pattern recognition.

xlix Ibid, 237.

l Ibid, 237-38.

li Ibid, 238.

lii Ibid, 238.

liii Ibid, 238-39.

liv Ibid, 239. The US Army prior to the Great War was not the most disciplined at times.

lv Ibid, 240-41.

lvi Ibid, 241-42.

lvii Ibid, 242-43.

lviii Ibid, 243-44.

lix Ibid, 244.

lx Ibid, 245.

lxi Ibid, 260.

lxii Ibid, 260-61.

lxiii Ibid, pg. 5.

lxiv Ibid, pg. 5.

lxv Frank Rzeczkowski, "The Crow Indians and the Bozeman Trail", 4-5.

lxvi Quoted in Hebard, Grace Raymond and E.A. Brininstool: *The Bozeman Trail, vol. 2*,121.

lxvii Ibid, 122.

lxviii John D. McDermott, "Red Cloud's War: The Bozeman Trail, 1866-1868", *The Western Historical Quarterly*, Vol. 42, Issue 4 (12/2011), pg. 8.

lxix Hebard, Grace Raymond and E.A. Brininstool: *The Bozeman Trail, vol. 2*, 140.

lxx Ibid p. 140. The Crow and Fort C.F. Smith's role in the Bozeman Trail's story will unfold in the next section.

lxxi John D. McDermott, "Red Cloud's War: The Bozeman Trail, 1866-1868", 10.

lxxii Hebard, Grace Raymond and E.A. Brininstool: *The Bozeman Trail, vol. 2*. Cleveland, The Arthur H. Clark Company, 1922, Kindle Edition, 2867-2909.

lxxiii John D. McDermott, "Red Cloud's War: The Bozeman Trail, 1866-1868", 10.

[lxxiv] Hebard, Grace Raymond and E.A. Brininstool: *The Bozeman Trail, vol. 2*, 175-176.

[lxxv] Ibid, 177.

[lxxvi] Ibid, 178. Red Cloud did not fight to the last, dying on a reservation in 1909.

[lxxvii] Ibid, 178.

[lxxviii] Frank Rzeczkowski, "The Crow Indians and the Bozeman Trail", 6.

[lxxix] Ibid, 6.

[lxxx] Ibid, 6.

[lxxxi] Ibid, 6.

[lxxxii] Ibid, 6.

[lxxxiii] Ibid, 6.

[lxxxiv] Ibid, 6-7.

[lxxxv] Ibid, 7.

[lxxxvi] Ibid, 7.

[lxxxvii] Ibid, 7. Context aside, it should again be noted the Crows would defend their lands against American incursions, as noted earlier.

[lxxxviii] Frank Rzeczkowski, "The Crow Indians and the Bozeman Trail", 7.

[lxxxix] Hebard, Grace Raymond and E.A. Brininstool: *The Bozeman Trail*, 228-229.

[xc] Ibid, 229.

[xci] Ibid, 230.

[xcii] Ibid, 230-31.

[xciii] Ibid, 231. The United States army refused to issue Remington rifles to the troops because they believed it would waste ammunition. This oversight would cost the United States dearly across the Plains. Obviously, the natives had no such qualms about purchasing the rapidly firing rifle.

[xciv] Frank Rzeczkowski, "The Crow Indians and the Bozeman Trail", 7.

[xcv] Hebard, Grace Raymond and E.A. Brininstool: *The Bozeman Trail*, 231-32.

[xcvi] Hebard, Grace Raymond and E.A. Brininstool: *The Bozeman Trail*, 232.

[xcvii] Frank Rzeczkowski, "The Crow Indians and the Bozeman Trail", 8.

[xcviii] Ibid, 8.

[xcix] Ibid, 8.

[c] Ibid, 8.

[ci] Ibid, 8.

[cii] Ibid, 9.

[ciii] Hebard, Grace Raymond and E.A. Brininstool: *The Bozeman Trail*, 343-344.

[civ] John D. McDermott, "Red Cloud's War: The Bozeman Trail, 1866-1868", 1.

[cv] Ibid 1.

[cvi] Ibid 1.

[cvii] Hebard, Grace Raymond and E.A. Brininstool: *The Bozeman Trail, vol. 2*, 43.

[cviii] Ibid, 43.

[cix] Ibid, 44.

[cx] Ibid, 44.

[cxi] Ibid, 46.

[cxii] Ibid, 46-47.

[cxiii] Ibid, 47.

[cxiv] Ibid, 48.

[cxv] Ibid, 48-49.

[cxvi] Ibid, 49.

[cxvii] Ibid, 49.

[cxviii] Ibid, 49.

[cxix] Ibid, 56-57.

[cxx] Ibid, 59-60.

[cxxi] Ibid, 66.

[cxxii] Ibid, 67.

[cxxiii] Ibid, 67.

[cxxiv] Ibid, 233-35.

[cxxv] Ibid, 235. The Blackfoot tribe roamed west of Pryor Creek.

cxxvi Frank Rzeczkowski, "The Crow Indians and the Bozeman Trail", 9.

cxxvii Hebard, Grace Raymond and E.A. Brininstool: *The Bozeman Trail*, 345.

cxxviii Frank Rzeczkowski, "The Crow Indians and the Bozeman Trail", 11.

cxxix Ibid, 11.

cxxx Ibid, 11.

cxxxi Ibid, 12.

cxxxii Ibid, 12.

cxxxiii Ibid, 12.

cxxxiv Ibid, 12.

cxxxv Ibid, 12.

cxxxvi Ibid, 12.

cxxxvii Ibid, 12.

cxxxviii Ibid, 12.

cxxxix Ibid, 13.

cxl Ibid, 13.

cxli Ibid, 13.

cxlii Ibid, 13. At this time, for comparison, a Sergeant in the Army made about $25 a month. Clearly, at least, the Crow had learned the civilizing power of capitalism.

cxliii Ibid, 13-14.

cxliv Ibid, 14.

cxlv Ibid, 14. Never mind the natives were winning the war, of course.

cxlvi Ibid, 14. Not that buffalo stuck around very long when Americans moved in –they all seemed to die from bullet wounds.

cxlvii Ibid, 14-15.

cxlviii Ibid, 15.

cxlix Ibid, 15.

cl Ibid, 15.

cli Ibid, 15.

clii Ibid, 15.

cliii Ibid, 15.

cliv Ibid, 15.

clv Ibid, 16.

clvi Ibid, 16.

clvii John D. McDermott, "Red Cloud's War: The Bozeman Trail, 1866-1868", 8.

clviii Ibid, 8.

clix "Treaty with the Sioux — Brulé, Oglala, Miniconjou, Yanktonai, Hunkpapa, Blackfeet, Cuthead, Two Kettle, Sans Arcs, and Santee — and Arapaho, 1868" (Treaty of Fort Laramie, 1868). 15 Stat. 635, Apr. 29, 1868. Ratified Feb. 16, 1868; proclaimed Feb. 24, 1868. In Charles J. Kappler, compiler and editor, Indian Affairs: Laws and Treaties — Vol. II: Treaties. Washington, D.C.: Government Printing Office, 1904, pp. 998-999.

clx Treaty of Fort Laramie, 1868, pg. 999-1002.

clxi Frank Rzeczkowski, "The Crow Indians and the Bozeman Trail", 16.

clxii Ibid, 16.

clxiii John D. McDermott, "Red Cloud's War: The Bozeman Trail, 1866-1868", 1.

clxiv Frank Rzeczkowski, "The Crow Indians and the Bozeman Trail", 17.

Made in the USA
Monee, IL
21 January 2021

58308263R00033